ALSO BY JOANNE WEIR

Weir Cooking: Recipes from the Wine Country

You Say Tomato

From Tapas to Meze

Seasonal Celebrations

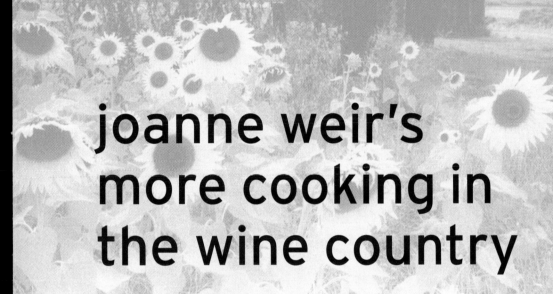

# joanne weir's more cooking in the wine country

## joanne weir

photographs by penina

simon & schuster

new york   london   toronto   sydney   singapore

SIMON & SCHUSTER
Rockefeller Center
1230 Avenue of the Americas
New York, NY 10020

Designed by Katy Riegel
Title page and running head art courtesy of PhotoDisc

Manufactured in the United States of America

10  9  8  7  6  5  4  3

Library of Congress Cataloging-in-Publication Data

Weir, Joanne.
    Joanne Weir's more cooking in the wine country / Joanne Weir.
       p.  cm.
    1. Cookery, American–California style. I. Title: More cooking in the wine country.
    II. Title.

TX715.2.C34 W44 2001                                        2001017019
641.59794–dc21
ISBN 0-7432-1251-7

To my father

# acknowledgments

**In the last year,** I have been touched by the support of my family and so many extraordinary friends. There have also been many wonderful people who have helped me with this cookbook and my TV series *Weir Cooking in the Wine Country II*. It is here that I wish to pay them tribute.

For her dedication, support, and superior editing abilities, I would like to thank Sydny Miner and the whole team at Simon and Schuster, especially Katy Riegel, Jonathon Brodman, and Kathy Ness. They not only kept up with the rigorous schedule, but they also kept me to mine. And to my agent, Doe Coover, I thank my lucky stars for putting me in good hands.

A special thanks to Penina, for her stunning photographs, along with Amy Nathan, for her impeccable detail and lovely styling, and Sara Slavin for her superb propping. All three of you put your hearts into this project and I appreciate it beyond words.

My special thanks to Barbara Ignatius for treating this book and the show as if they were her own. I couldn't have succeeded without her. "Do you have ten minutes?" Thanks to Lloyd Shupnik for his computer savvy. I would also like to thank recipe testers Kelly Molloy and Jean Tenanes for their hard work and attention to detail. For their friendship and loving support, my very best to Gary Danko, Laurence Jossel, and Bibby Gignilliat.

To the entire TV production team who swatted flies, tied scarves around their heads, gave me constant thumbs-up, and did a fantastic job, I would like to thank some of the most talented people in the field, my dear friend and producer Linda Brandt, director Bruce Franchini, art director

Bernie Schimbke, Tim Bellen, Steve Bellen, Allen Hereford, Nathan Williams, Mike Van Dine, Paul Swensen, Bruce Smith, Dwight Kiyono, Pat Sielski, Jill Kustner, Terrance Ranger, Lorraine Battle, Catherine Pantsios, Bruce Fielding, Kelly Molloy, Inge Scott, David Sanborn, Jim Dunn, Colleen Peterson, Elizabeth "Izzy" Swensen, Bernice Chuck Fong, Carol Odman, Leslie Typrin, and Jennifer Louie. To John Bayless, for being such a wonderful musician and sharing it with all of us every day.

To my dear friends Annie and Frank Farella, who let me think that their home is my own. To Tom Farella, for once again being the unsung hero. To Jean Tenanes, for the best chocolate cake a mother could make. To the best brother, John Tenanes, for being there when times are good and bad. Thanks to Peter Hall for sharing a picnic and the frenzy of shooting a show. To Jerry Comfort, Sue Conley, Evan Shively, David Goldman, and Lisa Court for adding spirit and life to the show.

To the entire staff of KQED, especially Regina Eisenberg and Shirley O'Neal for all their hard work and continued support. My heartfelt thanks.

To the people that make the show possible, thanks to the team at Sur La Table— Renee Benhke, Doralece Dullaghan, Susanna Linse. To everyone at Beringer Wine Estates—Walter Klenz, Tor Kenward, Brook Williams, Tracy Adamo. And to my friends at Calphalon—Jeff Cooley, Ann Jenkins, Paul Angelo Lo Giudice, Chris Tracy, Susan Doktor—and Cogent Public Relations.

To Caitlin Connelly, Ned Takahashi, Jim Brandt, Richard Poole, and Scott Griffin. For their generous support, Peet's Coffee and Tea, Manicaretti Imports, The Pasta Shop, Model Bakery, Oxo Good Grips, Melissa's World Variety Produce Inc., Dean and Deluca, and Scharffen Berger Chocolate Makers. Thanks to John and Patty Norton, John Dorenbecher, Nancy Gates, Earnest and Jean Vosti.

And to Paolo, thank you for making this year such a memorable one.

# contents

# foreword

## why i cook

**If I were to pick a place** on earth where the things that matter most to me about cooking take place, it would be the California wine country. In this sun-drenched valley, everything grows, something is always in season, and the habits of living are relaxed and celebratory.

It's easy to live the rich life here: eating fresh foods right out of the garden and orchard, savoring artisanal cheeses and breads, drinking vintage wines. When I'm here, I feel as though I'm living in a state of grace. There are unhurried lunches, dinners under the stars, an afternoon picnic along the roadside with a table and elegant linens. Improbably, in this age of hurry, there always seems to be enough time to linger at the table, talking over plates of simple food with friends or family.

Somehow, we all must eat. We can make indifferent meals, with little connection to where the food comes from. Or we can make meals that are cooked in harmony with the earth and with the seasons, and which are a recurring source of renewal, satisfaction, and celebration. The wine country just seems to require this kind of cooking, and that is part of why I love it.

I wasn't born here. I am a New Englander whose profession has allowed her to travel throughout the United States, Europe, the Middle East, and Australia, and who stumbled across this enchanted valley and found a culinary home. I spend as much time as I can here, though I do not live here year-round. But I have found that more than the valley's world-renowned wines can be imported wherever one lives.

When I travel, I pay attention to what is fresh, ripe, and ready to pick at each destination. If you think about it, that's part of what makes where you live special. Cooking and eating seasonally is to use what grows in the fields or migrates in the streams near your home, to use what is ripening on the trees or coming into bloom in the fields because that's what there is to cook with. It's wrapping fresh sprigs of thyme around the lamb for roasting because they come into their own at the same time of year; eating the cherries as fast as they ripen, baking them into warm clafoutis or layering them in a simple galette; it's making a summer salad of every variety, shape, and color of tomato or of all the stone fruits. It is making a celebration of the first ripe tomato. And even though we can now get almost anything in the way of foodstuffs any time of the year, there is something right in the juxtaposition of flavors that occurs naturally.

This emphasis on fresh ingredients and seasonality isn't meant to intimidate. You want to cook with and eat seasonal fresh food for what it brings to your life and because it connects you to the food—not because there is some edict to do so.

There are other ways to connect to the food we eat. I believe that the foods we love are imbued with story and memory. When I think about a great dish I had somewhere, it is always in the context of the people who made it for me or of some special feature of the place where I had it. I love to remember the people who prepared a certain dish or who inspired me to create a new one; you'll find some of their stories in this book.

As I travel, I've found that everyone has this connection to food. I have been privileged to meet people all over the world who have shared their stories with me and, when I am most lucky, shared their recipes. Sometimes it is in the form of a yellowed and torn handwritten recipe that was passed down from a grandparent or neighbor; other times it is a recipe that has been told and retold many times—an oral history. This is the cooking that interests me: food that has a story, that has meaning and vitality, that is alive with tradition.

I learned to cook by learning to love the time spent at the table in my parents' and grandparents' homes. They revered the table as the center of our family's life—as is the custom in Italy, where the family table is called *il sacro desco*. In my childhood home, my mother customarily prepared multicourse meals, and we all sat around the table talking, long after the last dishes had been cleared.

For me, food has always been about more than just eating. I cook as a way to nurture and nourish those at my table. Not just with food, but with a beautiful table set with flowers and good dishes so that, for this time at least, my guests are unhurried and alive to all their senses. I cook as a painter paints and a novelist writes—because it is the way I know to craft something of beauty.

I consider myself profoundly lucky to have found such a rewarding profession. I would love to inspire you to get back in the kitchen, to try new things, to cook more with seasonal ingredients.

This book will have accomplished its real purpose if I've instilled in you the zest and enthusiasm to fill your life with enjoyment, richness, friends and family, and to celebrate food and eating as we do in the wine country.

—Joanne Weir

Napa, California

June 2000

# joanne weir's more cooking in the wine country

# firsts

spiced bocconcini and tomatoes

garlic bruschetta

tomato bruschetta

grilled bread with fava beans and escarole

crostini with herbed goat cheese and wilted spinach

crostini with smoked trout and lemon zest

pita crisps with spinach, walnut, and garlic puree

endive with gorgonzola, caramelized onions, and fig jam

prosciutto-wrapped greens with hot pepper and garlic

rolled grape leaves with rice, feta, currants, and pine nuts

wilted greens with pine nuts, raisins, and fried bread

roasted potatoes with tomatoes and garlic mayonnaise

wood-fired vegetable salad with tomatoes, peppers, onions, and
olives

spanish omelette with smoked pimentos

sausage and pepper turnovers

pizza with leeks, gorgonzola, and walnuts

turkish pizza with red-hot spiced lamb and tomatoes

crispy cracker pizza with mahogany onions

calzone with four cheeses, eggplant, and basil

gorgonzola focaccia

fig and walnut flatbread

rice "olives"

risotto croquettes with mozzarella

risotto with zinfandel and radicchio

fettuccine with gorgonzola and pine nuts

red onion ravioli with thyme cream

semolina gnocchi with brown butter and crisp sage

scallop fritters with arugula salsa verde

garlic shrimp with romesco

hot crispy beets "in their jackets" with lemon mint aïoli

# the table

**I no longer think of the table** as a separate thing but instead as an integral part of our lives. Isn't it one of the few places where we ritually gather to be with one another? A good meal is always more than just the food and wine we eat and drink. It is also atmosphere, music, nice linens, flowers, and good dishes. In this sense, the table makes the first impression of a meal. But so does the first course.

*I primi piatti; antipasti; l'entrée; tapas; meȝe; mukabalatt.* By any name, I love them! Their job is simple: to delight and excite the palate, to set a mood, to extend our time at the table. How about a plate of shrimp with *romesco* sauce, endive with sweet caramelized onions, or *crostini* with fava beans and greens? I love to set out a whole group of first courses as a change from the usual sequence of first course, main dish, dessert. Sometimes I'll increase the serving size and make it a main course. And first courses make great picnic foods.

In the Mediterranean, the first course is very much a part of how people live. Families, friends, and coworkers gather in the evening to share small plates of simple, colorful, and flavorful food and to discuss the events of the day. I love bringing this custom to wherever I am, but especially to the wine country, where the Mediterranean sensibility is so easily evoked.

The first course is a savored one, and its memory lingers long after the plates have been cleared from the tables.

# spiced bocconcini and tomatoes

The great thing about antipasti is that they can be made as simple or as complex as you like. This simple antipasto pairs bite-size mozzarella balls (*bocconcini* means "small mouthfuls" in Italian) with cherry tomatoes. It takes two minutes to make and tastes great.

1 pound *bocconcini* (small mozzarella balls, 1-inch diameter)
2 cups assorted cherry tomatoes (red, yellow, orange, pear-shaped, grape-sized)
1 tablespoon chopped fresh oregano
¼ teaspoon crushed red pepper flakes
¼ cup extra virgin olive oil
Salt and freshly ground black pepper
Fresh oregano sprigs as a garnish

Place the mozzarella, tomatoes, oregano, red pepper flakes, and olive oil in a bowl. Gently stir together just until combined. Season with salt and pepper.

Spoon the mixture onto a platter, garnish with oregano sprigs, and serve.

Serves 6

Wine Suggestion: Pinot Noir or Shiraz

# tomato bruschetta

This is a dish to make at the height of summer, when we can celebrate the anniversary of that perfect marriage of basil and vine-ripened tomatoes. Just add a few drops of balsamic vinegar to bring out the sweetness of the tomatoes, and use a good coarse-textured, crusty bread for the *bruschetta*.

2 large ripe tomatoes, peeled, seeded, and cut into ½-inch dice

3 tablespoons extra virgin olive oil

½ teaspoon balsamic vinegar

Salt

6 slices coarse-textured country bread, cut ⅜-inch thick

2 large cloves garlic

10 fresh basil leaves

In a small bowl, toss together the tomatoes, 1 tablespoon of the olive oil, the balsamic vinegar, and salt to taste.

Under a broiler or on a wood-fired grill, toast the bread until golden on each side. Rub the bread lightly on one side with the garlic, using the toasted surface like a grater. With a pastry brush, brush on the remaining 2 tablespoons olive oil.

Pile the basil leaves on top of one another, roll them up, and cut into thin ribbons. Distribute the tomato mixture evenly over the toast, garnish with the basil, and serve immediately.

Serves 6

Wine Suggestion: Sauvignon Blanc

# how to peel, seed, and chop tomatoes

To peel tomatoes, begin by bringing a large pot of water to a boil. Submerge the tomatoes in the boiling water for 30 seconds. Then, using a slotted spoon, quickly remove the tomatoes from the water and plunge them into an ice-water bath. When they are cool enough to handle, core the tomatoes from the stem end, using a small paring knife. Then peel off the skins (they should come off easily; if not, return the tomatoes to the boiling water for a few seconds).

To remove the seeds, cut the tomatoes in half horizontally. Cup one half in your hand and, holding the tomato over a bowl, gently squeeze out the seeds (you can use your fingers to remove seeds from the cavity). Discard the seeds, skin, and core.

Chop the tomato in a rough dice using a sharp chef's knife.

# garlic bruschetta

The Italian word *bruschetta* is often mispronounced; it should be broo-*ske'*-tah. These toasts, rubbed with garlic and drizzled with olive oil, are a great way to salvage bread that is growing stale. Here I've made a *bruschetta* for garlic-lovers, utilizing both raw and roasted garlic for a double dose of the edible lily.

2 bulbs garlic

3 tablespoons extra virgin olive oil

Salt and freshly ground black pepper

1½ tablespoons chopped fresh flat-leaf parsley

1½ tablespoons finely chopped fresh chives

6 slices rustic country-style bread, cut ⅜-inch thick

2 cloves garlic

Fresh flat-leaf parsley sprigs as a garnish

Preheat the oven to 375°F.

Using a serrated knife, cut the top quarter off the bulbs of garlic. Place the bulbs in a small baking dish. Drizzle with the oil, season with salt and pepper, and cover with foil. Bake until the garlic is tender when pierced with fork, 30 to 40 minutes. Remove from the oven and let cool a bit.

Squeeze the base of the bulbs to extract as much of the garlic pulp from the skins as possible. Season the garlic to taste with salt and pepper, stir in the chopped parsley and chives, and reserve. Reserve the oil in the pan also.

Toast the bread on both sides, either over an outdoor grill, under the broiler, or in a toaster, until golden. Cut each piece of toast in half. Rub one side of the toasted bread with the whole cloves of garlic. Brush the toast with the reserved oil, and then spread the garlic paste over it.

Place the toasts on a platter. Garnish with sprigs of parsley, and serve immediately.

Serves 6

Wine Suggestion: Pinot Noir

# grilled bread with fava beans and escarole

I love fava beans, especially when I can get them fresh from the garden. Peeling and shelling fresh favas takes some work, but the payoff is so great that it's well worth the effort. In Italy, I have had fava beans when they were so tender and young that you could just pop them in your mouth without cooking. When the fava harvest is underway, the Italians love to celebrate by drizzling the fresh raw beans with fruity virgin olive oil, sprinkling them with sea salt, and shaving a bit of Parmigiano-Reggiano over the top.

Puréed with garlic and lemon and spread on grilled country bread, this is a great antipasto offering for a summer evening.

> 3 pounds fresh fava beans in the pod
>
> 1 clove garlic, minced
>
> 5 tablespoons extra virgin olive oil
>
> ½ tablespoon fresh lemon juice
>
> Salt and freshly ground black pepper
>
> 1 12-ounce bunch escarole, trimmed, cut into 1-inch-wide strips
>
> 1 tablespoon red wine vinegar
>
> Small pinch of crushed red pepper flakes
>
> 24 slices country-style bread, cut ⅜-inch thick, grilled or toasted
>
> 3 ounces Pecorino cheese
>
> Lemon wedges as a garnish

Shell the beans and discard the pods. Bring a saucepan three-quarters full of water to a boil. Add the beans and cook over medium-high heat for 30 seconds. Drain the beans, reserving 1 cup of the cooking liquid. Let the beans cool for 10 minutes. Then pop the skins off the beans.

Place the beans, garlic, and 2 tablespoons of the olive oil in a skillet. Over medium-high heat, cook the beans, stirring frequently and adding the reserved cooking liquid as necessary to form a rough paste, 20 minutes. Remove the beans from the heat and

# how to peel fava beans

Fava beans first begin to appear in the market in mid-spring, their large thick pods a brilliant green. As the season progresses and the beans mature, the pods may be splotched with black and the flavor of the beans may become more pronounced. Fava beans are also known as broad beans or horse beans and have a flat, kidney-shaped appearance.

To prepare fava beans, first remove the beans by snapping the pods where you feel a bean and popping out the beans. If the beans are very small, about the size of a large pea, you can eat the bean and pod raw, or you can blanch them in boiling water for 10 seconds.

When the beans are larger, it is best to remove the skin. To do this, bring a pot of water to a boil. Add the fava beans and blanch them for 20 to 25 seconds. Immediately remove them with a slotted spoon. Plunge into ice water to cool. When the beans have cooled enough to handle, make a small slit with your fingernail in the side of the skin and pop the bean out. Discard the skins.

pulse the mixture in a food processor or blender to form a smooth paste. Stir in the lemon juice, 2 tablespoons of the olive oil, and salt and pepper to taste.

In another skillet, heat the remaining 1 tablespoon olive oil over high heat. Add the escarole and cook, tossing frequently with kitchen tongs, until it wilts, 2 to 3 minutes. Toss in the vinegar, red pepper flakes, and salt and pepper to taste.

Spread the bean puree on the grilled bread and top with the wilted escarole. With a cheese shaver or vegetable peeler, shave a few thin slices of Pecorino onto the top of each piece. Garnish with lemon wedges and serve immediately.

**Makes 24 pieces; serves 8**
**Wine Suggestion: Pinot Noir**

# crostini with herbed goat cheese and wilted spinach

During the holidays about ten years ago, I began to wish that there was an office Christmas party for me to go to. Realizing that I had a number of friends who were similarly self-employed, I planned a get-together that has now become a tradition. Each year, we gather for a multi-course luncheon, which I cook. Last year I started lunch with these *crostini* and a glass of Champagne.

6 ounces or 1¼ cups fresh goat cheese, room temperature

1 tablespoon grated lemon zest

2 tablespoons thinly sliced fresh chives

1 tablespoon chopped fresh flat-leaf parsley

1 tablespoon chopped fresh mint

2 teaspoons chopped fresh oregano

1 teaspoon chopped fresh thyme

Salt and freshly ground black pepper

1 tablespoon extra virgin olive oil

½ pound fresh baby spinach leaves, washed, stems trimmed

6 slices rustic country-style bread, cut ⅜-inch thick

In a bowl, mash together the goat cheese, lemon zest, chives, parsley, mint, oregano, thyme, and salt and pepper. Reserve.

In a large frying pan, warm the olive oil over medium-high heat. Add the spinach, and using tongs, toss the spinach until wilted, 2 to 3 minutes. Season to taste with salt and pepper. Set aside.

Toast the bread on an outdoor grill, under the broiler, or in a toaster. Cut each slice in half on the diagonal.

Spread the herbed goat cheese evenly over the toasted bread. Top the goat cheese with the wilted spinach, distributing it evenly. Place the grilled bread on a platter, and serve immediately.

Serves 6

Wine Suggestion: Sauvignon Blanc

# crostini with smoked trout and lemon zest

When I want a simple dish to serve with drinks, especially Champagne or sparkling wine, this is one of my favorite choices. It's really best with homemade mayonnaise, but you can use store-bought. Smoked trout is available at most grocery stores, but you could also substitute any smoked fish.

¼ cup mayonnaise

2 small cloves garlic, minced

1½ teaspoons fresh lemon juice

1 teaspoon grated lemon zest

⅛ teaspoon cayenne pepper

½ teaspoon sweet paprika

2 scallions, white and green parts, thinly sliced

Salt and freshly ground black pepper

1½ cups flaked smoked trout (3 ounces), bones removed

18 slices rustic coarse-textured bread, cut into 2½-inch squares, ½-inch thick

1 ounce caviar (American sturgeon, salmon, osetra, beluga, or sevruga)

Lemon wedges as a garnish

In a small bowl, combine the mayonnaise, garlic, lemon juice, lemon zest, cayenne, paprika, and scallions. Season to taste with salt and pepper. Mix well. Add the trout and stir to combine.

Grill or toast the bread. Spread the trout mixture on top of the toasted bread squares. Garnish each one with a dollop of caviar, and serve immediately with lemon wedges alongside.

**Serves 6**

**Wine Suggestion: Chardonnay, Viognier, sparkling wine, or Champagne**

# pita crisps with spinach, walnut, and garlic puree

Pita chips are like an edible spoon and may be served with all kinds of pastes, purees, and salads. They're simple to prepare and just as good made ahead as they are fresh. (Store them in an air-tight container for up to three days.) I love them with this simple first course, or *meze*, which comes from Volos, on the coast of Greece, where my friend Stavoula gave me the recipe. The puree is similar to, but not as traditional as, the classic *skorthalia*, a pungent garlic dip that's thickened with toasted walnuts, potatoes, and/or stale bread. (There is a version of *skorthalia* with the Batter-Fried Crispy Fish in the Mains chapter.)

> 3 pita breads (8-inch diameter)
> 9 tablespoons extra virgin olive oil
> Salt
> 1 cup fresh spinach, washed and coarsely chopped
> ½ cup fresh bread crumbs
> ¼ cup cold water
> ¾ cup plus 2 tablespoons walnut halves
> 3 cloves garlic, minced
> 2 teaspoons fresh lemon juice
> Salt and freshly ground black pepper
> Lemon wedges as a garnish

Preheat the oven to 375°F. Separate each pita bread into 2 rounds, and cut each round into 8 wedges. Place the wedges on a baking sheet. Drizzle with 3 tablespoons of the olive oil, sprinkle with salt, and toss together. Bake in the oven, tossing occasionally, until crisp, 10 to 12 minutes. Remove from the oven and let cool on the baking sheet. Leave the oven on.

Bring a pot of salted water to a boil. Add the spinach to the boiling water and immediately drain it. Pat it dry with paper towels.

Soak the bread crumbs in the cold water, and then squeeze them well to remove the excess moisture. Discard the water.

Place the walnuts on a baking sheet and bake in the oven until they are golden, 7 minutes. Chop enough of the walnuts to make 2 tablespoons, and set aside.

Combine the spinach, bread crumbs, remaining walnut halves, remaining 6 tablespoons olive oil, garlic, and lemon juice in a blender or food processor. Blend to create a smooth paste. Taste, and season with salt and pepper.

Mound the puree on a plate, and sprinkle it with the reserved chopped walnuts. Garnish with lemon wedges, and serve with the pita crisps.

**Makes 48 pita crisps and 1½ cups puree; serves 8**

**Wine Suggestion: Pinot Noir**

# endive with gorgonzola, caramelized onions, and fig jam

This elegant first course was inspired by Bibby Gignilliat, a great cook, wonderful assistant, and good friend. Bibby layers the Gorgonzola, onions, and fig jam on grilled bread. I wanted to lighten the recipe a bit, so I put them on endive leaves. It's terrific both ways!

If you don't want to make your own jam, you can buy fig jam at specialty markets.

> 3 tablespoons extra virgin olive oil
> 3 yellow onions, thinly sliced
> ½ teaspoon sugar
> ½ teaspoon minced fresh thyme
> Salt and freshly ground black pepper
> 4 large heads Belgian endive
> 4 ounces Italian Gorgonzola cheese, crumbled
> G cup Black Mission Fig Jam (recipe follows)

Warm the olive oil in a large skillet over moderate heat. Add the onions, sugar, and thyme. Cook, stirring occasionally, until the onions are a caramel color and very soft, 30 to 40 minutes. Season with salt and pepper. (This mixture can be made a day in advance and refrigerated. Bring to room temperature before filling the leaves.)

Cut ½ inch off the bottom of each head of endive. Discard the outer leaves. Separate the leaves and discard the small inner leaves (or reserve them for another purpose). You should have approximately 36 leaves. (You can store the leaves in a single layer under damp towels for up to 4 hours.)

Fill the base of each endive leaf with the caramelized onion mixture, distributing it evenly. Top each one with 1 teaspoon Gorgonzola and a dollop of the fig jam. Arrange on a platter and serve.

**Makes 36 pieces**
**Wine Suggestion: Shiraz**

# black mission fig jam

You can substitute other varieties of fresh figs.

20 fresh black Mission figs (about 1½ pounds), stemmed and cubed
½ cup honey
¼ cup water
1 tablespoon fresh lemon juice

In a medium saucepan, combine the figs, honey, water, and lemon juice. Bring the mixture to a simmer over medium heat and cook, stirring occasionally, until thick, 20 minutes. Test the jam by spooning a little onto a chilled saucer; place the saucer in the freezer for a few minutes; the mixture should firm up to a thick jamlike consistency.

Remove the jam from the heat and let it stand for 5 minutes. Then spoon it into hot sterilized glass jars to within ½ inch from the top. Place the lids and rings on the jars and seal tightly. Let cool completely. Refrigerate for up to 3 months.

**Makes 2 to 2½ cups**

# prosciutto-wrapped greens with hot pepper and garlic

This antipasto comes from my days at Chez Panisse. The pieces are like little cigars, with the prosciutto rolled up around the wilted greens. The great thing is that this simple dish incorporates so many flavors: sweetness and acidity from the balsamic vinegar, saltiness from the prosciutto, bitterness from the greens, and hotness from the pepper.

6 cups trimmed assorted greens (Swiss chard, escarole, mustard greens, beet greens, chicory, radicchio), stems removed

3 tablespoons extra virgin olive oil

2 cloves garlic, minced

2 to 3 teaspoons red wine vinegar

Pinch of crushed red pepper flakes

Salt and freshly ground black pepper

18 thin slices prosciutto

Arrange the greens in piles, roll them up, and cut them into 1-inch-wide strips. Wash them well and spin dry.

Heat the olive oil in a large skillet over medium-high heat. When it is hot, add the greens and garlic and toss for 2 to 4 minutes until the greens have wilted but are still bright green. Reduce the heat to low and continue to cook until soft, 2 minutes. Taste, and add the vinegar and red pepper flakes. Season with salt and pepper.

Lay one slice of prosciutto flat on a work surface. Place 2 to 3 tablespoons of the wilted greens at one end of the slice. Roll the prosciutto up completely to form a cigar shape. Repeat with the remaining prosciutto and greens.

Arrange on a platter and serve.

Makes 18 rolls; serves 6
Wine Suggestion: Shiraz

# rolled grape leaves with rice, feta, currants, and pine nuts

In Greece, *dolmades* are traditionally made with ingredients like lamb and rice or raisins. I've given them a new twist here by adding feta cheese. When you're cooking them, be sure to use lots of fruity extra virgin olive oil and lemon juice.

1 jar (16 ounces) preserved vine leaves, or 50 pesticide-free fresh young vine leaves

¾ cup extra virgin olive oil

2 yellow onions, minced

⅓ cup pine nuts

1 cup chopped scallions, white and green parts

1 cup long-grain white rice

¼ cup chopped fresh parsley

¼ cup chopped fresh mint

¼ cup chopped fresh dill

⅓ cup dried currants

2 cups water

½ teaspoon salt

Freshly ground black pepper

6 ounces feta cheese, crumbled

12 sprigs fresh dill

Pinch of salt

½ cup fresh lemon juice

Lemon wedges as a garnish

Bring a large pot of salted water to a boil. Rinse the preserved vine leaves and blanch them, a few at a time, in the boiling water for 30 seconds. If you are using fresh grape leaves, blanch them for 2 to 3 minutes in the boiling water. Using a slotted spoon, transfer the leaves to a bowl of ice water and let them cool. Drain the leaves and cut off the tough stems.

Heat ½ cup of the olive oil in a large skillet over medium heat. Cook the onions, stirring occasionally, until soft, 7 minutes. Reduce the heat to low and add the pine nuts, scallions, and rice. Stir for 2 minutes. Then stir in the parsley, mint, dill, currants, 1 cup of the water, the ½ teaspoon salt, and pepper to taste. Cover and cook until the rice is tender and the water has been absorbed, 15 minutes. Remove from the heat and allow to cool. Add the feta and stir together.

To stuff the grape leaves, place a leaf, smooth side down, on a work surface. Place a heaping teaspoon of the filling near the base of the leaf, at the stem end. Fold the stem end and sides over the filling and roll toward the point of the leaf, making a little bundle. Repeat with the remaining leaves and filling.

Line the bottom of a heavy 4-quart saucepan with the dill sprigs. Sprinkle with a pinch of salt. Pack a layer of the rolls in close together, seam side down. Combine the remaining ¼ cup olive oil and the lemon juice. Sprinkle the layer of rolls generously with some of the olive oil/lemon mixture. Repeat, layering the rolls and sprinkling with the oil/lemon mixture. Add the remaining 1 cup water and cover the rolls with a few additional vine leaves. Invert a small heatproof plate on top to keep the rolls in shape. Cover the saucepan tightly and bring to a boil. Turn the heat down to low, and simmer until the vine leaves are tender, 1½ hours.

Remove the pan from the heat and let sit until the liquid is absorbed, about 2 hours. Serve warm or at room temperature, garnished with lemon wedges.

**Makes 60 rolled grape leaves**

**Wine Suggestion: Sauvignon Blanc**

# wilted greens with pine nuts, raisins, and fried bread

Long ago, this *tapa* was made in Spain with wild greens that were foraged from nearby fields. I like to make it with spinach, which pairs wells with the sweetness of the raisins. You could also substitute Swiss chard, beet or dandelion greens, or escarole.

½ cup pine nuts

3 large bunches (36 ounces) spinach or Swiss chard

1 teaspoon water

Salt and freshly ground black pepper

¼ cup golden raisins

¼ cup dark raisins

1 cup boiling water

¼ pound stale (3-days-old) coarse-textured bread, crusts removed

5 tablespoons extra virgin olive oil

3 cloves garlic

1 clove garlic, minced

4 anchovy fillets, soaked in cold water for 10 minutes and patted dry

Warm a small skillet over medium heat. Add the pine nuts and stir until golden, 2 to 3 minutes. Set aside to cool.

Remove the stems from the greens. Wash the greens well and pat dry. Heat a large skillet over medium heat. Add the greens and the 1 teaspoon water, season with salt and pepper, and cover. Cook, tossing occasionally, until wilted, 3 minutes for spinach and 6 to 8 minutes for Swiss chard. Set aside.

Combine the raisins in a heatproof bowl. Pour the boiling water over them, and let stand for 15 minutes. Drain, and set aside.

Heat the oven to 350°F.

Tear the bread into rough 1-inch pieces, or cut into 1-inch cubes.

Warm 3 tablespoons of the olive oil in a skillet over medium heat, add the garlic cloves and cook for 1 minute, until golden. Remove the garlic. Sauté the bread pieces in the oil until golden and crisp. Season with salt and pepper.

Heat the remaining 2 tablespoons olive oil in a large skillet over low heat. Add the minced garlic and cook, stirring constantly, for 30 seconds. Mash the anchovies and add them to the garlic. Stir until dissolved. Add the pine nuts, raisins, wilted greens, and salt and pepper to taste. Toss together and place on a platter. Garnish with the fried bread and serve warm.

**Serves 6**

**Wine Suggestion: Sauvignon Blanc**

# roasted potatoes with tomatoes and garlic mayonnaise

In Spain, this popular dish goes by the name *patatas brava*, a bow to its fiery flavor. The degree of spiciness depends on where it's made: the farther south you go, the hotter it seems to get!

3 pounds small red potatoes, unpeeled, cut in half

2 tablespoons extra virgin olive oil

Salt and freshly ground black pepper

¼ cup minced yellow onion

2 cloves garlic, minced

2 cups peeled, seeded, chopped tomatoes, fresh or canned

1 tablespoon tomato paste

½ cup dry white wine

1 cup water

¼ teaspoon crushed red pepper flakes

½ teaspoon Tabasco sauce

1 bay leaf

2 tablespoons chopped fresh flat-leaf parsley

¼ teaspoon chopped fresh thyme

Pinch of sugar

2 to 3 teaspoons red wine vinegar

1 recipe Allioli (recipe follows)

Preheat the oven to 375°F.

Toss the potatoes, 1 tablespoon of the olive oil, and salt and pepper to taste in a baking dish. Arrange the potatoes in a single layer in the dish, and bake on the top shelf of the oven until golden and cooked through, 45 minutes.

Meanwhile, heat the remaining 1 tablespoon olive oil in a skillet over medium-low heat. Add the onions and garlic, and cook until soft, 7 minutes. Add the tomatoes, tomato paste, white wine, water, red pepper flakes, Tabasco, bay leaf, parsley, thyme, and sugar.

Season to taste with salt and pepper. Simmer until the sauce thickens slightly, 20 minutes. Cool for 10 minutes. Then remove the bay leaf and puree the sauce in a blender until smooth. Stir in the vinegar, and season with salt and pepper to taste.

Place the warm potatoes on a serving dish, and pour the tomato sauce over them. Drizzle the Allioli over the top, and serve immediately.                                   Serves 8

Wine Suggestion: Chardonnay


## allioli

½ cup corn, peanut, or canola oil

½ cup extra virgin olive oil

1 egg yolk, room temperature

5 cloves garlic

Salt

1 to 1½ tablespoons white wine vinegar or fresh lemon juice

Freshly ground black pepper


Combine the two oils in a liquid measuring cup.

Place the egg yolk in a bowl and mix well with 1 tablespoon of the combined oil until an emulsion is formed. Drop by drop, add the remaining oil to the emulsion, whisking constantly. Continue to do this in a fine steady stream, whisking, until all of the oil has been added. Do not add the oil too quickly, and be sure that the emulsion is homogeneous before adding more oil. Mash the garlic with a pinch of salt in a mortar and pestle, or finely mince the garlic. Add the garlic to the mayonnaise. Add the vinegar, and season with salt and pepper.                                   Makes about 1 cup

*Note: This garlic mayonnaise can be made up to 6 hours ahead of time and stored, covered, in the refrigerator.*

*The use of raw eggs carries the risk of salmonella poisoning. Foods containing raw eggs should not be eaten by the very young, the very old, pregnant women, or anyone with a compromised immune system.*

# strawberry sangría

I have a real soft spot for the small plates of the Mediterranean, so much so that my first book, *From Tapas to Meze*, was devoted entirely to them. So when my dear friend Laurence Jossel opened Chez Nous in San Francisco, I was first at the door. Along with his delicious *tapas* and *meze*, he serves a luscious sangría that he changes with the season. This one is perfect for spring. In the summer Lawrence substitutes ripe peaches for the strawberries and uses fruity white wine in place of the red; and in the winter, he adds all kinds of citrus.

> 1 bottle (750 ml) fruity red wine
> 1 pound fresh strawberries (about 2 pints), hulled and sliced
> 1 cup fresh apple juice
> ⅓ cup Triple Sec liqueur
> ¼ cup sugar (more or less depending upon the ripeness of the berries)
> 2 whole cloves
> 1 cinnamon stick (3 inches)

Combine all the ingredients in a large pitcher. Stir until the sugar dissolves. Cover and refrigerate for at least 4 hours or up to one day. Remove the cloves and cinnamon stick. Pour the sangría into glasses, being sure to include some of the strawberries. Serve with a spoon to eat the fruit.

Serves 8

# wood-fired vegetable salad with tomatoes, peppers, onions, and olives

In Spain this smoky-flavored salad is called *escalivada,* from the Catalan word *escalivar,* which means "to cook in hot embers" or "to roast." Using typical Mediterranean ingredients like peppers, onions, tomatoes, garlic, eggplant, and olives, plus a liberal dose of olive oil, it's not unlike France's *ratatouille* or Italy's *caponata.* It's best made in the late summer or early fall, when the harvest vegetables are at their peak.

1½ pounds eggplant, preferably long thin ones

5 small (1 to 1¼ pounds) ripe red tomatoes

1 large red bell pepper

1 large green bell pepper

2 small yellow onions

4 tablespoons extra virgin olive oil

2 cloves garlic, minced

3 tablespoons chopped fresh flat-leaf parsley

18 oil-cured black olives

Start a wood or charcoal grill. (Alternatively, the vegetables can be charred under the broiler or directly over a gas burner.)

Preheat the oven to 350°F. Wash and dry the eggplant, tomatoes, and bell peppers. Peel the onions.

Set the grill rack 4 inches from the heat source. Grill the eggplant, tomatoes, bell peppers, and onions over a very hot fire, turning occasionally, until the vegetables are black on all sides, 5 to 7 minutes.

Brush 1 tablespoon of the oil over the vegetables. Cut the tomatoes and the onions in half, and place them in a roasting pan so that the tomatoes are cut side up and the onions are cut side down. Add the eggplant and bell peppers to the pan, and put the pan in the oven. The tomatoes will cook in approximately 15 minutes; the bell peppers

and eggplant will take 15 minutes; and the onions will be done in 1 hour. Remove the vegetables as they are done.

When the vegetables are done, place them, still hot, in a plastic bag, seal, and let stand for 15 minutes. Then remove them from the bag. Core, seed, and peel the peppers; slice into thin strips. Peel the eggplant and tear into thin strips. Slice the onions. Slip the tomatoes out of their skins and cut in half.

Arrange the vegetables in rows on a serving dish, alternating the colors. Season with salt and pepper, and drizzle with the remaining 3 tablespoons olive oil. Combine the parsley and garlic, and chop together until very finely minced. Sprinkle this mixture over the vegetables. Garnish with the olives, and serve.

Serves 6 to 8

Wine Suggestion: Dry rosé

## roasting bell peppers

Preheat the broiler.

Cut the bell peppers in half and place them, cut side down, on a baking pan. Broil the peppers until they are completely black, 6 to 10 minutes. (Alternatively, pierce the whole pepper with a long-handled fork and hold it directly over the burner on a gas stove, or place it on a wood-fired or charcoal grill, turning it occasionally until the skin is completely black on all sides, 5 to 6 minutes.)

Place the charred peppers in a paper or plastic bag, close the bag, and let them steam for 10 minutes. When the peppers are soft, remove them from the bag, and using a knife, scrape off and discard the black skin. (I don't recommend peeling them under running water since some of the flavor is lost that way.)

If you haven't already done so, cut the peppers in half. Remove and discard the stem, membrane, and seeds.

# spanish omelette with smoked pimentos

The Spanish name for this *tapa* is *tortilla español*. It's made with pimentón powder, a variety of paprika that gives off a slightly smoky flavor that is great with the sweetness of fresh or roasted pimento or red bell peppers. You can find it at well-stocked specialty stores.

> 1 cup olive oil
>
> 3 small baking potatoes, cut into ½-inch wedges or chips
>
> Salt and freshly ground black pepper
>
> 6 eggs
>
> 1 pimento pepper or red bell pepper, roasted (see page 44) and cut into ½-inch dice
>
> ½ teaspoon pimentón powder (optional)

Heat the olive oil in a 10-inch nonstick omelette pan over medium heat. Add the potatoes in layers, seasoning with salt and pepper as you add them. Cook slowly over medium heat, moving the potatoes occasionally, until they are tender but not brown, 10 to 15 minutes. The potatoes should be separate and not in a cake. Drain the potatoes, reserving 3 tablespoons of the oil. Let the potatoes cool completely.

In a large bowl, beat the eggs until foamy. Add the potatoes, pimento, and pimentón powder. Season with salt and pepper to taste. Mix thoroughly, until the potatoes are completely covered with egg. Let the mixture sit for 15 minutes.

Return the reserved 3 tablespoons oil to the omelette pan and heat over medium-high heat, just until the oil begins to ripple. Reduce the heat to medium. Pour the eggs/potato mixture into the pan and cook over medium heat. Using a spatula or fork, loosen the edges of the tortilla and allow some of the runny mixture to flow down the sides. When the tortilla is almost firm and golden on the first side (after about 15 minutes), invert a large plate over the pan. Wearing oven mitts, invert the plate and pan together. Slide the tortilla off the plate back into the pan, browned side up. Cook until done, 5 minutes. It should be slightly juicy inside. Let the tortilla cool for 15 minutes.

Cut into wedges and serve warm or at room temperature.

**Serves 8 to 10**

**Wine Suggestion: Pinot Noir**

# olive oil

I love olive oil. It is in my trinity of revered ingredients, right up there with tomatoes and garlic.

My reverence dates to a trip I made many years ago to Nyons, in the south of France, where I had gone on a kind of food tour. Nyons is a village known for its olives and olive oil production. When I arrived, the air itself seemed scented with olive oil. The harvest was in, and all over, freshly picked olives were being ground and pressed into the most wonderful fruity olive oil.

Nowadays I can find thirty to forty different varieties of olive oil from half a dozen countries at my market. There are inexpensive bottles of "pure" olive oil, usually a blend of refined and virgin oils, and special bottles of extra virgin olive oil that can cost a hundred dollars or more. And flavored olive oils abound—lemon, tangerine, hot red pepper, porcini mushroom, garlic, even Tahitian lime!

I like to use fruity, peppery, complex extra virgin olive oil for dressings, pastas, and simple dishes in which its flavors can really be appreciated. Pure olive oil is good for frying and for use with delicate foods that might be overpowered by a stronger-tasting oil. I think it's worthwhile to buy the best olive oil you can and to experiment with ones you haven't had before.

Perhaps, then, you will come to love it as I do.

# sausage and pepper turnovers

I can never have this Spanish *tapa*—called an *empanadita,* or "little turnover"—without remembering the great and inventive cook who served it to me. Beatriz Tamarit and her husband, Jose Luis, had invited me to their home in southern Spain on a cool November evening. When we sat at the table for this first course, my hosts covered their laps with the overhanging edges of the tablecloth. I followed their lead and discovered that the tablecloth was heated, like an electric blanket! The turnovers were wonderful and I was warm.

1 tablespoon extra virgin olive oil

1 small yellow onion, cut into ¼-inch dice

½ green bell pepper, cut into ¼-inch dice

2 cloves garlic, minced

½ pound pork sausage or chorizo, casings removed, chopped

Large pinch of saffron threads

½ cup peeled, seeded, chopped tomatoes, fresh or canned

¼ cup finely chopped green olives stuffed with pimento

½ teaspoon ground cumin

1 hard-boiled egg, finely chopped

Salt and freshly ground black pepper

1 recipe Quick Puff Pastry (recipe follows), or 1½ pounds frozen puff pastry, thawed

1 egg, whisked

1 tablespoon water

Warm the olive oil in a frying pan over medium heat. Add the onions, bell peppers, and garlic, and cook, stirring occasionally, until the onions and peppers are soft, 10 minutes. Add the sausage and cook, stirring occasionally, until it has rendered some of its fat, 5 minutes.

Heat a small skillet over medium heat, and add the saffron. Cook, shaking the pan frequently, for 30 seconds. Add the saffron, tomatoes, olives, and cumin to the sausage and simmer, covered, for 10 seconds. Remove the cover and continue to cook

until the moisture evaporates, 3 to 4 minutes. Add the hard-boiled egg and mix well. Season with salt and pepper, and set aside.

Preheat the oven to 350°F.

On a floured surface and using a floured rolling pin, roll the puff pastry out to ⅛-inch thickness. Using a 3½-inch round cookie cutter or a clean empty can, cut out as many circles as possible. Place a tablespoon of the filling to the side of the center of each circle. Combine the whisked egg with the water. Brush the edges of the circles with this egg wash. Fold each circle over to form a half-moon, enclosing the filling. Press the edges to seal them. Place the turnovers on an ungreased baking sheet, and bake until golden brown, 15 minutes.

Arrange the turnovers on a platter and serve hot, warm, or at room temperature.

Makes 24 turnovers

Wine Suggestion: Merlot

## quick puff pastry

I haven't made traditional puff pastry for years! Instead, I use this quick version that incorporates all of the turns at one time, yielding a fine-quality pastry with much less work. It will take you only about fifteen minutes to prepare, but be sure to thoroughly chill the butter and flour in the freezer before making the dough.

2⅔ cups all-purpose flour
½ teaspoon salt
1½ cups (3 sticks) unsalted butter
1½ tablespoons fresh lemon juice
⅔ cup ice water

Mix the flour and salt together and chill in the freezer for 1 hour before using. Cut the butter into ¼-inch dice and chill in the freezer for 1 hour.

Place the cold flour on a work surface. Add the butter, and using a pastry scraper, cut half of the butter into the size of peas and the other half smaller than peas. (Alternatively, you can pulse this mixture in a food processor to the same point; then dump the mixture onto the work surface.)

This next step needs to be done on the work surface: Combine the lemon juice and ice water in a small pitcher. Add the liquid little by little to the flour mixture, stirring, using as much liquid as needed until the dough is moistened and just beginning to hold together. The mixture should still be cold. Press the dough together as best you can to form a rough rectangle.

There will be large chunks of butter showing. Do not knead the dough. Roll the dough out to form a ½-inch-thick rectangle with one of the short sides close to you. Fold the short ends toward the center so they meet in the center. Fold in half again so that there are four layers. This is your first turn.

Turn the dough a quarter turn and roll it again to form a ½-inch-thick rectangle. Repeat the folding process. This is your second turn.

Turn the dough a quarter turn and roll it again to form a ½-inch-thick rectangle. This time, fold it into thirds as you would a business letter. Wrap the dough in plastic wrap and refrigerate it for 1 hour.                    **Makes 1½ pounds**

*Note: The dough can be stored in the refrigerator for up to 3 days. It can also be kept frozen for 1 month.*

# pizza with leeks, gorgonzola, and walnuts

During the time I worked at Chez Panisse, we must have made over five hundred different kinds of pizzas. This might seem like a strenuous undertaking, but what I loved about Chez Panisse was that pizza was not just about tomatoes and cheese. It was an opportunity for invention and for finding new and interesting mixes of flavor and texture. For this pizza, the sweetness of stewed leeks, some Gorgonzola cheese to add flavor and body, and the slightly bitter taste of walnuts makes a great combination.

1 recipe The Best Pizza Dough (recipe follows)

4 tablespoons extra virgin olive oil

5 large leeks, white part and 1 inch of green, thinly sliced, washed well and drained

Salt and freshly ground black pepper

2 cloves garlic, minced

½ cup (2 ounces) fontina cheese, freshly grated

½ cup (2 ounces) mozzarella cheese, freshly grated

¾ cup (3 ounces) Gorgonzola cheese, crumbled

½ cup walnut halves

Make the pizza dough and let it rise for a minimum of 1 hour and up to 2 hours.

Thirty minutes before baking, place a pizza stone on the bottom shelf of the oven and set the oven temperature to 500°F.

In a large frying pan over medium heat, warm 2 tablespoons of the olive oil. Add the leeks and cook, stirring occasionally, for 5 minutes. Reduce the heat to low, cover, and continue to cook, stirring occasionally, until the leeks are soft, 25 to 30 minutes. Remove the cover and cook until the leeks are soft and falling apart, 10 minutes. Season with salt and pepper, and set aside.

In a small bowl, combine the garlic with the remaining 2 tablespoons olive oil, and let stand for 30 minutes. In another bowl, combine the fontina, mozzarella, and Gorgonzola, and reserve.

In the meantime, place the walnuts on a baking sheet and bake until light golden, 2 to 3 minutes. Chop very coarsely.

Punch down the dough. On a floured surface, divide the dough into 2 pieces and form them into round balls. Roll one piece of dough out to form a 9-inch circle, ¼-inch thick. Transfer it to a well-floured pizza peel or paddle. Brush some of the garlic-infused oil over the dough to within ½ inch of the edge. Spread half of the cheese

# what you need to make great pizza or calzone at home

It is so easy to make good pizza or calzone at home in your own oven! There are only a few things to remember, and they apply to both pizza and calzone. (Whenever I say pizza, I will mean calzone too.)

First, you need an oven that reaches at least 500°F. Ideally you want the temperature between 500° and 700°F, so the hotter your oven the better, just like a wood-fired pizza oven in Italy.

Next, you need a pizza stone or unglazed quarry tiles, which you set on the bottom shelf of the oven. If you are using quarry tiles, push them together so you have enough surface to set the pizza on top. Remember—and this is very important—to heat the pizza stone or quarry tiles to the oven's hottest temperature for at least 30 minutes before you place the pizza in the oven. Don't even think about putting your pizza onto a cold stone! It would defeat the whole purpose of the stone.

Last, you need a pizza peel or paddle, preferably made of wood, to lift the pizza in and out of the oven. Once you make the dough, place it on the well-floured peel. When the pizza stone is hot, transfer the pizza from the peel to the stone, holding the peel at a 20° angle, touching the tip of the peel to the stone as you slide the pizza off the peel directly onto the stone. Bake until golden and crisp.

mixture on top of the oil. Distribute half of the leeks over the cheese, spreading them out evenly. Sprinkle with half of the walnuts. Slide the pizza onto the heated pizza stone and bake until golden and crisp, 8 to 12 minutes. Remove the pizza from the oven and serve immediately. Continue with the remaining ingredients to make a second pizza.

Makes two 9-inch pizzas

Wine Suggestion: Merlot or Shiraz

## the best pizza dough

2 teaspoons dry yeast

¾ cup plus 2 tablespoons lukewarm water (100°F)

2 cups unbleached bread flour

2 tablespoons olive oil

½ teaspoon salt

In a bowl, combine the yeast, ¼ cup of the lukewarm water, and ¼ cup of the flour. Let it stand until it bubbles up, a minimum of 30 minutes or up to 1 hour.

Add the remaining ½ cup plus 2 tablespoons lukewarm water, the remaining 1¾ cups flour, the olive oil, and the salt. Mix the dough thoroughly. Turn it out onto a floured surface and knead until smooth, elastic, and a bit tacky to the touch, 7 to 8 minutes.

Place the dough in an oiled bowl and turn to cover it with the oil. Cover with plastic wrap and let rise in a warm place (75°F) until doubled in volume, 1 to 1½ hours. (Alternatively, let this dough rise in the refrigerator overnight. The next day, bring the dough to room temperature and proceed.)      Makes dough for two 9-inch pizzas

# turkish pizza with red-hot spiced lamb and tomatoes

I like to think of this as an Arab version of an Italian pizza. It is inspired by *lahmaçun*, which means "dough with meat," a Middle Eastern dish. Here I put the traditional topping of lamb, tomatoes, and spices on a pizza.

4 tablespoons extra virgin olive oil

2 cloves garlic, minced

1 cup (4 ounces) fontina cheese, coarsely grated

½ cup (2 ounces) mozzarella cheese, coarsely grated

1 small onion, finely chopped

½ pound ground lamb

½ cup peeled, seeded, chopped plum tomatoes, fresh or canned

1 tablespoon tomato paste

3 tablespoons chopped fresh parsley

3 tablespoons pine nuts, toasted (see page 154)

Large pinch of ground cinnamon

Large pinch of ground allspice

Large pinch of ground cloves

⅛ teaspoon crushed red pepper flakes

1 to 2 teaspoons fresh lemon juice

Salt and freshly ground black pepper

1 recipe The Best Pizza Dough (see page 54)

Place a pizza stone or quarry tiles on the bottom shelf of the oven, and preheat the oven to its hottest temperature setting, at least 500°F.

Combine 2 tablespoons of the olive oil with the garlic in a small bowl, and let sit for 30 minutes.

Combine the two cheeses in a small bowl, and set aside.

Heat the remaining 2 tablespoons olive oil in a large skillet, and sauté the onions until soft, 10 minutes. Add the lamb, tomatoes, tomato paste, parsley, pine nuts, and spices, and cook slowly, uncovered, for 10 minutes. Add the lemon juice and mix well. Season to taste with salt and pepper. Remove from the heat.

Punch down the dough. On a floured surface, roll one half of the pizza dough out to form a 9-inch circle, ¼-inch thick. Transfer it to a heavily floured pizza peel. Brush some of the garlic oil over the dough to within ½ inch of the edge. Sprinkle half of the cheese mixture on top, and then half of the spiced lamb mixture. Slide the pizza onto the heated stone, and bake until golden and crisp, 8 to 10 minutes. Remove the pizza from the oven and serve immediately. Repeat with the remaining ingredients to make a second pizza.

**Makes two 9-inch pizzas**

**Wine Suggestion: Pinot Noir or Cabernet Sauvignon**

# crispy cracker pizza with mahogany onions

*Pissaladière* with a twist! Here I've updated the traditional Provençal onion and anchovy "pizza." The onions are double-caramelized until they acquire a rich mahogany color, and the crust is rolled very thin and cooked until crisp like a cracker. (To get the crust so thin, you must allow the dough to rest between rolling. This takes some patience, but it allows the gluten in the dough to relax so that the dough can be rolled thin.) I like to serve this pizza hot, sliced in wedges, with wine or drinks before a meal.

**Dough:**

¾ cup lukewarm water (110°F)

2 teaspoons dry yeast

2 cups unbleached bread flour

3 tablespoons extra virgin olive oil

½ teaspoon salt


Topping

6 red onions, unpeeled

2 tablespoons extra virgin olive oil

1 teaspoon salt

Freshly ground black pepper

1 teaspoon dried oregano

1 tablespoon dried thyme

1 tablespoon light brown sugar

¼ cup balsamic vinegar

Salt

4 anchovy fillets, soaked in cold water for 10 minutes and patted dry, mashed

6 tablespoons freshly grated Parmigiano-Reggiano cheese


Combine ¼ cup of the lukewarm water, the yeast, and ¼ cup of the flour in a bowl. Let stand for 30 minutes, until it bubbles. Add the remaining ½ cup lukewarm water, the remaining 1¾ cups flour, and the olive oil and salt. Mix the dough thoroughly.

Knead the dough on a floured board until it is soft but still moist, 7 to 10 minutes. Place it in an oiled bowl, turning it once to cover it with oil. Cover the bowl with a kitchen towel and put it in a warm place (75°F). Let the dough rise until it has doubled in volume, 1 hour. (After the dough has doubled in volume, it can be stored in the refrigerator for up to one day. Bring the dough to room temperature before rolling.)

In the meantime, heat the oven to 375°F. Prepare the topping: Halve the onions from top to bottom, but do not peel them. In a baking pan, toss the onions with the oil, the 1 teaspoon salt, pepper to taste, and the oregano and thyme. Place the onions on a baking sheet, cut side down, and cook until they are completely soft, 50 to 60 minutes. Remove from the oven. When the onions are cool enough to handle, peel them and cut them into thin slices. Place them in a skillet over low heat, add the brown sugar and vinegar, and mix well. Cook uncovered, stirring occasionally, until mahogany brown and almost dry, 50 minutes. Season with salt and pepper to taste. When the onions have cooled, add the anchovies and mix well. (The onions can be prepared one day in advance and stored in the refrigerator.)

Place a pizza stone or quarry tiles on the bottom shelf of the oven, and preheat the oven to 500°F, or higher if possible, for at least 30 minutes.

Punch down the dough. On a floured surface, divide the dough into 2 pieces and shape each one into a smooth round cake. With a floured rolling pin, roll one piece of dough out on a floured surface, resting for a few minutes and then rolling again, until it forms a 12-inch circle, ⅛-inch thick. Spread half of the onions evenly over the top, leaving a ½-inch border around the edge. Bake until crisp and light golden, 6 to 9 minutes. Remove from the oven, sprinkle with half of the Parmigiano, and serve immediately. Continue with the reamining ingredients to make a second pizza.

Makes two 12-inch pizzas

Wine Suggestion: Pinot Noir

# calzone with four cheeses, eggplant, and basil

*Calzone* literally means "trouser leg"; the great half-moon of pastry is filled with everything from ricotta and mozzarella to sausage and salami. Calzone originated in Naples and are a favorite in New York City, but it's easy to make them at home. They're baked on a pizza stone just like a pizza and can be made in large or individual-size servings.

2 cloves garlic, minced

4 tablespoons extra virgin olive oil

¾ pound small Japanese eggplant, cut into 1/4-inch thick slices

Salt and freshly ground black pepper

1 tablespoon balsamic vinegar

¼ cup pine nuts

1 red bell pepper, cut into thin strips

1 recipe Calzone Dough (recipe follows)

¼ cup grated Parmigiano-Reggiano cheese

1¼ cups (about 5 ounces) grated fontina cheese

1¼ cups (about 5 ounces) grated mozzarella cheese

¾ cup (about 3½ ounces) crumbled goat cheese

20 large fresh basil leaves, cut into thin strips

Fresh basil sprigs as a garnish

Place a pizza stone on the bottom shelf of the oven, and preheat the oven to 400°F for at least 30 minutes. Meanwhile, combine the garlic and olive oil in a small bowl and let stand for 30 minutes.

Brush the eggplant slices with 2 tablespoons of the garlic olive oil, coating both sides. Place the slices in a single layer on a baking sheet and bake, turning occasionally, until tender, 10 to 15 minutes. Season with salt and pepper. Toss the eggplant with ½ tablespoon of the balsamic vinegar, and reserve.

Heat a medium-size frying pan over medium heat. Add the pine nuts and stir constantly until golden, 2 to 3 minutes. Remove from the pan and reserve. Add 1 table-spoon of the garlic olive oil to the same pan and place it over medium heat. Cook the bell peppers until soft, 10 minutes. Season with salt and pepper and the remaining ½ tablespoon balsamic vinegar. Set aside.

Increase the oven temperature to 500°F.

On a floured surface, roll half of the dough out to form a 12-inch circle, about ¼-inch thick. Place it on a well-floured pizza peel. Brush the dough lightly to within 1 inch of the edge with the remaining garlic olive oil. Combine the Parmigiano, fontina, mozzarella, and goat cheese in a bowl, and toss to mix. Spread half of the cheese mixture over half of the dough, leaving a 1-inch border. Arrange half of the eggplant slices, bell peppers, pine nuts, and basil over the cheese.

With a pastry brush, moisten the bottom edges of the dough lightly with water, and fold the dough over the filling so that a bit of the bottom edge is showing. Fold the bottom edge up over the top edge, crimping as you go so you have a tight seal. Slide the calzone onto the stone and bake until golden and crisp, 12 to 15 minutes. Remove from the oven and serve on a wooden cutting board, garnished with basil sprigs.

Repeat with the remaining dough and filling ingredients to make a second calzone.

Makes 2 large calzone; serves 4

Wine Suggestion: Pinot Noir or Chianti

## calzone dough

2½ teaspoons (1 package) dry yeast

¼ cup lukewarm water (about 110°F)

2¾ cups all-purpose flour

½ teaspoon salt

1 teaspoon extra virgin olive oil

1 cup water

Combine the yeast, lukewarm water, and ¼ cup of the flour in a large bowl. Let sit until it bubbles up, at least 20 minutes and up to an hour.

Add the remaining 2½ cups flour and the salt, olive oil, and 1 cup water. Mix well with a wooden spoon. When the dough forms a ball, turn it out onto a floured work surface and knead the dough until it is smooth, elastic, and a bit tacky and slightly sticky to the touch, about 10 minutes. Place the dough in an oiled bowl and turn it to coat the top with oil. Cover the bowl with plastic wrap and let the dough rise in a warm place (about 75°F) for a minimum of 1 hour or up to 2 hours, or until nearly doubled in volume. Punch down the dough and use.     **Makes 2 large or 4 small calzone**

# gorgonzola focaccia

The word *focaccia* comes from *focolare*, "the hearth"–where it used to be baked. Like pizza, *focaccia* is a thin flatbread made all over Italy that can be covered with many different toppings. This *focaccia* was inspired by one an Italian friend served in her home. Not only is it a great combination of flavors, but the Gorgonzola filling is incredibly creamy. My friend's secret is to mash the Gorgonzola with butter.

> 3 tablespoons plus ⅓ cup warm water (about 115°F)
> 1 teaspoon dry yeast
> 1¾ cups all-purpose flour
> ½ teaspoon salt
> 2 tablespoons extra virgin olive oil
> 1½ tablespoons pine nuts
> ¾ cup (3 ounces) Gorgonzola cheese, room temperature
> 2 tablespoons unsalted butter, room temperature
> ¼ small red onion, very thinly sliced

Combine the 3 tablespoons warm water, the yeast, and ¼ cup of the flour in a bowl. Let the mixture stand until it bubbles up, 20 to 30 minutes. Add the remaining ⅓ cup warm water and the salt, olive oil, and the remaining 1½ cups flour. Mix the dough well and form it into a ball. Knead the dough on a floured surface until it is smooth, elastic, and still moist, about 10 minutes. Place it in an oiled bowl, turning once to cover the top with oil. Cover the bowl with plastic wrap and put it in a warm place (about 75°F) until the dough has doubled in volume, a minimum of 1 hour and up to 2 hours.

Place a pizza stone on the bottom shelf of the oven, and preheat the oven to 500°F for at least 30 minutes.

Heat a dry frying pan over medium heat, add the pine nuts, and cook, stirring constantly, until golden, 2 to 3 minutes. Reserve.

Divide the dough into 2 pieces and form each into a round ball. On a well-floured surface, roll one piece of the dough out to form a 10 x 12-inch rectangle, ⅛-inch thick. Transfer the dough to a well-floured pizza peel and arrange it so that the longer side is closest to you. In a small bowl, mash the Gorgonzola, butter, and pine nuts together. Spread half of the cheese mixture over the right-hand half of the dough, leaving a 1-inch border around the edge. Spray or brush the edges of the dough lightly with water. Fold the empty half of the dough over the filled half, and press the edges together, enclosing the cheese. Trim the edges with a sharp knife. Score the top of the dough in three or four places with 1-inch slits. Scatter half of the onion slices over the top of the flatbread. Repeat with the remaining dough and filling ingredients. Transfer the flatbreads to the pizza stone and bake until lightly golden, 5 to 7 minutes. Serve immediately.

**Makes 2 flatbreads; serves 6**

**Wine Suggestion: Cabernet Sauvignon**

# fig and walnut flatbread

Not only is this flatbread beautiful to look at, it also has great texture: light on the inside and crisp on the outside. It is cooked with onions, figs steeped in Marsala, and walnuts. The figs give off a wonderful smoky flavor that goes well with the bitterness of the walnuts. I love to serve this hot from the oven. It would be great in the fall, alongside onion soup or a salad containing goat cheese or Stilton with a little walnut oil in the dressing.

**Dough**

¼ cup extra virgin olive oil

3 sprigs fresh rosemary

2½ teaspoons (1 package) dry yeast

½ cup plus 2 cups unbleached bread flour

½ cup lukewarm potato water or plain water (110°F; see Note, page 67)

1 teaspoon coarsely chopped fresh rosemary

½ cup potato water

1 teaspoon salt

**Topping**

6 to 8 dried figs, sliced

1 cup Marsala wine

3 tablespoons extra virgin olive oil

1 red onion, cut into ½-inch-thick vertical slices

1 tablespoon sugar

½ teaspoon grated orange zest

Salt and freshly ground black pepper

¾ cup walnut halves

In a small saucepan, warm the olive oil and rosemary. Remove from the heat and let cool for 1 hour. Discard the rosemary sprigs.

In a large bowl, mix together the yeast, ½ cup flour, and ½ cup warm potato water.

# zinfandel

Zinfandel is an exotic black grape variety of European origin that is culti-vated primarily in California. It was first brought to the U.S. by George Gibbs, of Long Island, who obtained it from an imperial nursery in Vienna around 1829. Although he originally brought them to Boston, within thirty years Zinfandel grapes were being grown in both Napa and Sonoma coun-tries. It became the regular drink of the miners and other participants in the California Gold Rush. By the 1880s the grape had secured its place in the California wine business by virtue of its ability to produce in quantity. By the turn of the century, Zinfandel was considered California's own claret.

Although Zinfandel is much revered by some and underestimated by others, the grape is capable of producing excellent wines. Its flavor is classically claret-like; it should have a really lush berry flavor and spici-ness with a reasonable amount of tannin (though not as much as a Caber-net Sauvignon).

For this reason, Zinfandel would be good with steak, venison, sausage, or the Fig and Walnut Flatbread.

Let stand 1 hour, until it bubbles up and rises. Then add the remaining 2 cups flour, rosemary olive oil, chopped rosemary, potato water, and salt. Mix the dough thor-oughly. Knead the dough on a floured board until it is soft but still moist, 7 to 8 min-utes. Place the dough in an oiled bowl, turning it once to cover it with oil. Cover the bowl with plastic wrap and put it in a warm place (about 75°F). Let the dough rise for 1 to 2 hours, until doubled in volume.

In the meantime, prepare the topping: Place the figs and Marsala in a saucepan, and

heat over medium heat until the Marsala bubbles around the edges, 1 minute. Remove from the heat and let stand for 1 hour.

Heat the olive oil in a large frying pan over medium heat. Add the onions and sugar and cook, stirring occasionally, until the onions are very soft, 15 to 20 minutes. Add the orange zest, season with salt and pepper, and set aside to cool.

Place a pizza stone on the bottom shelf of the oven, and preheat the oven to 500°F for 30 minutes.

Form the dough into a round ball. Let it rest for 5 minutes. On a floured surface, roll the dough out to form a 9 x 12-inch oval, ½-inch thick. Place it on a well-floured pizza peel. Drain the figs and distribute the figs, onions, and walnuts evenly over the *focaccia*. Lightly press them into the dough. Let it rest for 10 minutes. Then transfer the *focaccia* to the pizza stone and bake until golden brown and crispy, 12 to 15 minutes. Serve immediately.               Makes 1 *foccacia;* serves 6

Wine Suggestion: Chianti, Zinfandel, Riesling, or Gewürztraminer


*Note: The potato water called for here is the water left after boiling peeled and quartered russet potatoes. Drain and mash the potatoes for dinner, or use them for another purpose, and reserve the water.*

# rice "olives"

I absolutely love these bite-size antipasti. The idea for them came from Gabrielle Feron, a good friend who lives in the Veneto, where her family has grown rice for generations. The "olives" are made with risotto that is flavored with olive paste and then shaped into small balls, breaded, and deep-fried. Just pop them in your mouth.

2 tablespoons extra virgin olive oil

½ small onion, minced

1 cup arborio, vialone nano, or carnaroli rice

1¼ cups chicken stock

1¼ cups milk

⅔ cup olive paste (see Note)

Salt and freshly ground black pepper

½ cup finely grated Parmigiano-Reggiano cheese

1 cup all-purpose flour

4 eggs

½ cup water

4 cups toasted finely ground fresh bread crumbs

Mixture of vegetable and olive oil for deep-frying

Heat the olive oil in a skillet over medium-low heat. Add the onions and sauté until soft, 7 minutes. Add the rice and continue to cook, stirring constantly, for 3 minutes.

Meanwhile, combine the chicken stock and milk in a saucepan and heat just to a simmer.

Immediately add the simmering liquid, ⅓ cup of the olive paste, and salt and pepper to taste to the rice. Bring to a simmer, reduce the heat to low, cover, and cook slowly until the rice is cooked, 20 minutes. Stir in the remaining ⅓ cup olive paste and the Parmigiano. Let cool completely.

Place the flour in a bowl. Whisk the eggs and water together in another bowl. Place the bread crumbs in a third bowl. Season each of the three bowls with a pinch of salt.

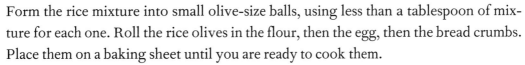

Form the rice mixture into small olive-size balls, using less than a tablespoon of mixture for each one. Roll the rice olives in the flour, then the egg, then the bread crumbs. Place them on a baking sheet until you are ready to cook them.

Heat 1 inch of oil to 375°F in a deep heavy pan.

Fry the rice olives, a few at a time, in the hot oil until golden on all sides, 60 to 90 seconds. Remove, and serve immediately.

**Makes 50 balls; serves 12**

**Wine Suggestion: Cabernet Sauvignon**

*Note: Olive paste, or olivada, can be found in jars in specialty markets.*

## making fresh bread crumbs

Place the bread in the food processor and process until finely ground.

## making toasted or dry bread crumbs

Preheat the oven to 375°F.

Place the fresh bread crumbs on a baking sheet and bake, tossing occasionally, until golden, 10 to 15 minutes.

# risotto croquettes with mozzarella

In northern Italy, they call these *suppli al telefono*—"telephone wires." The name comes from the long strands of mozzarella that you see when you break apart these wonderful risotto croquettes. In southern Italy they are called *arancini*, meaning "orange," because they look like the fruit.

**3 cups chicken stock**

**1¼ cups water**

**2 tablespoons extra virgin olive oil**

**1 small onion, minced**

**1½ cups arborio, vialone nano, or carnaroli rice**

**½ cup tomato sauce, fresh or canned**

**1 cup grated Parmigiano-Reggiano cheese**

**1 egg yolk, beaten**

**Salt and freshly ground black pepper**

**¼ pound fresh whole-milk mozzarella cheese, cut into ¼-inch dice**

**Corn or peanut oil for deep-frying**

**3 eggs, beaten**

**2 cups fine dry bread crumbs**

Combine the chicken stock and 1 cup of the water in a saucepan, and bring to a boil on the back burner of the stove. Reduce the heat to low and maintain below the boil.

Warm the olive oil in a large, heavy flameproof casserole over medium heat. Add the onions and cook until soft, 7 minutes. Add the rice and stir to coat it with the oil and heat it through, 2 to 3 minutes. Add about 1 cup of the hot broth and cook, stirring the rice constantly to wipe it away from the bottom and sides of the pot. When more than half of the broth has been absorbed but the rice is still loose, add another ladle of broth and continue to cook the rice. Continue to add broth, a ladle at a time, stirring constantly and letting it become absorbed, until the rice is chalky in the center, 15 to 18 minutes. (If you run out of broth, use hot water.) Continue to add broth until the center of the rice is tender and no longer chalky, about 3 to 5 minutes. Continue to cook a little more until the

# risotto

Here's a trick for making the perfect risotto that I learned in the Veneto, where they grow great rice. I've never read it or heard it before. Once the risotto is beyond the chalky stage, cook it 2 to 3 minutes more until it loses all its chalkiness. Take it off the heat, and add the butter, grated Parmigiano, another ladle of broth, and any other flavorings your recipe calls for (e.g., shrimp, zucchini). Give it a little stir; put the cover back on, and let it sit for 5 minutes off the heat.

While the risotto sits, get your guests to the table. Give the risotto a last stir, and serve.

rice is dry. Add the tomato sauce and Parmigiano, and stir together. Let cool completely. Add the egg yolk and mix well. Season with salt and pepper.

Using a small ice cream scoop or a dessert spoon, scoop up about ¼ cup of the rice mixture. Push two fingers into the mixture to make a small opening, and put 1 tablespoon of the mozzarella in the hole. Close the hole and finish shaping the croquette by hand to form a small egg shape. Repeat with the remaining rice and mozzarella. Set the croquettes on a baking sheet as you form them.

Heat 3 inches of oil to 375°F in a deep heavy saucepan.

Place the eggs and the remaining ¼ cup water in a bowl, and whisk together. Place the bread crumbs in a second bowl and season with salt and pepper. Roll the *suppli* in beaten egg first, and then in the bread crumbs. Set them on a cookie sheet lined with parchment or waxed paper. Deep-fry the *suppli,* a few at a time, in the hot oil, turning them occasionally, until golden brown, 1 to 2 minutes. Remove with a slotted spoon and drain on paper towels. Serve hot, warm, or at room temperature.

Makes 24 croquettes; serves 8
Wine Suggestion: Shiraz or Chianti

# risotto with zinfandel and radicchio

La Foresteria is an old hunting lodge outside Verona that has been converted to an exquisite inn. I teach there each year. The lodge was built by the descendants of Dante Alighieri, the Italian poet and author of *The Divine Comedy*. One of the traditional dishes of that region is Risotto with Amarone. It inspired this version, where I use Zinfandel rather than Amarone—the results are just as impressive.

3 tablespoons extra virgin olive oil

1 small yellow onion, diced

2½ cups chicken stock

1½ cups water

2 cups red Zinfandel wine

2 cups vialone nano or arborio rice

2 tablespoons unsalted butter

Freshly grated nutmeg

1 cup grated Parmigiano-Reggiano cheese

1 small head radicchio, halved and cut into thin strips

Salt and freshly ground black pepper

Heat the olive oil in a large heavy pot over medium heat. Add the onions and cook, stirring occasionally, until soft, 10 minutes.

In the meantime, combine the chicken stock and water in a saucepan and bring to just below a simmer on the back burner of the stove. In another saucepan, warm the wine to just below a simmer.

Add the rice to the onions and stir until it is very hot, just beginning to stick to the bottom of the pan, and completely coated with oil, 2 to 3 minutes. Add 2 ladlefuls of hot red wine and stir constantly until the wine is almost absorbed. Add a ladleful of chicken broth and stir steadily to keep the rice from sticking. Continue to add the broth a little at a time, stirring until it is absorbed. Then continue with the wine. Continue to add the wine until the rice is at the chalky stage, 18 to 22 minutes. Then continue to add wine and stir for an additional 2 minutes, until it is just beyond the chalky stage. (If you run out of red wine, use hot water.)

Remove the pan from the heat, and add another ladleful of red wine or water. Add the butter, nutmeg to taste, ½ cup of the Parmigiano, the radicchio, and salt and pepper to taste. Stir quickly. Cover and let sit, off the heat, for 5 minutes.

Stir the risotto and scatter with Parmigiano. Serve immediately with more Parmigiano on the side.

Serves 8

Wine Suggestion: Zinfandel or Shiraz

# rich homemade chicken stock

5 pounds chicken parts, backs, necks, wings, breast bones, excess fat removed

1 onion, peeled and coarsely chopped

1 carrot, peeled and coarsely chopped

12 parsley stems

½ teaspoon fresh or dry thyme

2 bay leaves

Place all of the ingredients in a stock pot. Add water to 2 inches over the bones. Bring to a boil and immediately reduce heat to a simmer. Simmer slowly until the meat has fallen off the bone and the stock tastes very rich, 5 to 6 hours. As the level of the liquid decreases in the pot, replenish it periodically to maintain the original level.

Strain the stock through a fine-mesh strainer into a bowl. Place in the refrigerator and allow the stock to cool completely. When it has cooled, remove the fat from the top with a spoon.

Makes 8 to 12 cups

# fettuccine with gorgonzola and pine nuts

Made with heavy cream, Gorgonzola, and Parmigiano-Reggiano, this dish is a cholesterol night-mare! But if you adhere to the edict "Everything in moderation" and don't eat all of it yourself, you will surely enjoy this richly satisfying dish. And it's so simple to make.

1 cup heavy cream

½ cup pine nuts

½ cup mascarpone cheese

6 ounces Gorgonzola cheese

½ cup grated Parmigiano-Reggiano cheese

Salt and freshly ground black pepper

1 pound fettuccine

2 tablespoons chopped fresh flat-leaf parsley

Bring the cream to a boil in a small saucepan, and cook until the quantity is reduced by one third, 5 to 10 minutes.

Meanwhile, warm a small, dry skillet over medium heat. Add the pine nuts and stir until golden, 2 to 3 minutes.

In a bowl, mix the reduced cream with the mascarpone, Gorgonzola, and Parmigiano. Place in a saucepan and heat gently. Season with salt and pepper, and stir in the pine nuts.

Bring a large pot of salted water to a boil. Add the pasta and cook until al dente. Drain, and toss with the sauce. Place on a platter, garnish with the parsley, and serve.

Serves 6

Wine Suggestion: Cabernet Sauvignon

# red onion ravioli with thyme cream

I don't know why it is, but I love making and eating ravioli. I've been cooking this dish for years. I roast the red onions in their skins with some fresh thyme and oil and then deglaze the pan with balsamic vinegar. The sauce is made with cream reduced with fresh thyme.

8 small red onions

2½ tablespoons olive oil

1 teaspoon salt

Freshly ground black pepper

2 tablespoons finely chopped fresh thyme

2½ tablespoons balsamic vinegar

2 pounds Fresh Egg Pasta Dough (recipe follows)

2 cups heavy cream

8 sprigs fresh thyme

1 cup grated Parmigiano-Reggiano cheese

Preheat the oven to 375°F.

Trim and halve the onions. Do not peel them. In a flameproof baking pan, toss the onions with the oil, 1 teaspoon salt, pepper to taste, and the thyme. Roast the onions, cut side down, in the oven until they are very soft and the skins are brown, about 1 hour. Remove the onions from the pan and allow to cool. Add the balsamic vinegar to the baking pan, and place the baking pan directly on a gas or electric burner. Reduce, stirring constantly, over medium-high heat until less than 1 tablespoon remains. Reserve.

When the onions are cool enough to handle, peel and chop them. Place them in a bowl with the reserved pan juices, and season with salt and pepper.

Cut the dough into 4 pieces. Using a hand-cranked pasta machine, open the rollers to the widest opening. Roll 1 piece of dough through the pasta machine 4 times, dusting with flour and folding the dough in half each time. Adjust the rollers to the next notch and roll the dough through once, dusting with flour. Continue to roll, adjusting the rollers until the dough is approximately ⅙-inch thick and you can almost see your hand through the dough.

Place the sheet of pasta on a well-floured work surface. Spoon a heaping teaspoon of onion filling at one end, just below the center of the dough. Continue to place mounds of filling all the way down the dough, leaving approximately 1½ inches between each mound. With a spray bottle filled with water, spray the edges lightly. Fold the top half of the dough over the onions to encase the filling and seal around the edges.

With a zigzag roller or knife, trim the long side close to the edge of the dough and discard. Cut in between each ravioli. Place on a floured kitchen towel set on a baking sheet.

For the thyme cream: Put the cream and thyme sprigs in a saucepan and cook until the cream is slightly thickened, 5 to 10 minutes. Strain. Taste, and season with salt and pepper as needed. Rewarm before serving.

To cook the ravioli: Bring a large pot of salted water to a boil and carefully add the ravioli. When they are cooked to al dente, 3 to 5 minutes, immediately remove them from the water and drain thoroughly. Gently toss the ravioli with the thyme cream and the grated Parmigiano. Serve immediately.       **Makes 48 ravioli; serves 8**

**Wine Suggestion: Chardonnay or Pinot Noir**

## fresh egg pasta dough

2 cups all-purpose flour

¼ teaspoon salt

2 eggs

1 tablespoon water

In the bowl of a food processor, pulse together the flour and salt. Add the eggs and water, and process until the dough forms a soft ball but is not sticky. If it is sticky, add more flour, a tablespoon at a time. Remove the dough from the processor bowl and knead it on a very lightly floured board until soft and smooth, 2 to 3 minutes. Let the dough rest, wrapped in plastic wrap, for at least 30 minutes.

Roll as needed.       **Makes approximately 1 pound pasta**

# semolina gnocchi with brown butter and crisp sage

Each year, I teach a couple of weeklong cooking courses in Italy. During one of the classes in a tiny hilltop village in Umbria, Giovanna Ancari came in and made these gnocchi, a dish traditionally made in Rome. At the risk of sounding like a cooking teacher, I will warn you: if you don't season the gnocchi with plenty of salt and nutmeg, they won't work—the flavor will just fall flat. So make sure you taste!

4 cups milk

1 cup semolina flour

9 tablespoons unsalted butter

1 cup grated Parmigiano-Reggiano cheese

Freshly grated nutmeg

1 egg, whisked

Salt

Olive oil

50 fresh sage leaves

Place the milk in a heavy saucepan and heat it to scalding. Whisking, add the semolina slowly. Change to a wooden spoon and stir until stiff and thick and the wooden spoon stands up by itself when set in the center of the gnocchi mixture, 20 minutes. Add 3 tablespoons of the butter, ½ cup of the Parmigiano, nutmeg to taste, the egg, and salt to taste. Stir well until the butter has melted.

Spread the dough out with a rubber spatula on a wet surface to ¾-inch thickness. Allow it to cool at least 1 hour, or up to 3 days in the refrigerator.

Preheat the oven to 425°F.

Using a 2-inch round cookie cutter, cut out as many circles of dough as possible. Butter a 13 x 9-inch baking pan. Arrange the circles, overlapping, in rows in the pan. Melt the remaining 6 tablespoons butter in a small saucepan until a light brown nutty color, 2 to 5 minutes. Drizzle the browned butter evenly over the gnocchi. Sprinkle the remaining ½ cup Parmigiano over the top. Bake until the gnocchi are light golden, 25 minutes.

In the meantime, heat about ½ inch of olive oil in a small skillet until it begins to ripple. Add the sage leaves in batches, and cook until deep green and crisp, 30 seconds. Remove the leaves from the pan with a slotted spoon or tongs, and drain on paper towels.

Place the gnocchi on plates, garnish with the sage leaves, and serve.    **Serves 8**

**Wine Suggestion: Merlot**

# scallop fritters with arugula salsa verde

*Salsa verde* just means "green sauce." In Italy, *salsa verde* is traditionally made with parsley, all kinds of different herbs, lemon, olive oil, and capers. In this version, I've used arugula, which gives the sauce a peppery, nutty quality. This sauce is so good, it can be used on anything from chicken and fish to veal or even pork chops. The scallops can be replaced with any other shellfish—shrimp, clams, or mussels.

1 cup all-purpose flour

½ teaspoon salt

2 eggs, separated

2 tablespoons olive oil

¾ cup warm (room-temperature) beer

1 pound sea scallops, muscle removed and discarded

Salt and freshly ground black pepper

½ cup coarsely chopped fresh arugula

¼ cup chopped fresh flat-leaf parsley

3 tablespoons chopped fresh chives

½ teaspoon chopped fresh thyme

½ teaspoon chopped fresh oregano

3 tablespoons capers, rinsed and chopped

1 shallot, minced

1 teaspoon grated lemon zest

1 clove garlic, minced

3 tablespoons fresh lemon juice

⅓ cup extra virgin olive oil

4 cups corn or peanut oil for deep-frying

Lemon wedges as a garnish

Sift the flour and ½ teaspoon salt into a large bowl. Beat the egg yolks in a small bowl. Make a well in the center of the flour mixture, and add the egg yolks, olive oil, and beer. Whisk just until the mixture is blended. Do not overmix. Let the batter rest for 1 hour at room temperature.

Cut the scallops into ½-inch pieces and place them in a bowl. Season with salt and pepper. Cover and reserve in the refrigerator.

Prepare the *salsa verde:* In a bowl, mix together the arugula, parsley, chives, thyme, oregano, capers, shallots, lemon zest, garlic, lemon juice, and olive oil. Season with salt and pepper. Use this within 1 hour.

Heat the corn or peanut oil to 375°F in a deep heavy pot. The oil should sizzle when you drop in a bit of the batter. Beat the egg whites in a bowl until they form stiff peaks. Fold the whites into the batter. Add the batter to the scallops and stir gently to combine.

Drop heaping tablespoons of the batter into the hot oil, and cook until golden brown, 30 to 60 seconds. Drain on paper towels. Place the fritters on a platter and garnish with lemon wedges. Place the *salsa verde* in a small bowl and serve it alongside.

**Serves 6**

**Wine Suggestion: Sauvignon Blanc**

# garlic shrimp with romesco

This is a typical first course in Tarragona, in northeastern Spain. The shrimp are sautéed quickly in olive oil and garlic and then served with a delicious *romesco* sauce. *Romesco* is great with this or any kind of fish or chicken. In Spain I have even seen it served with a combination of grilled leeks and scallions. I like to put it on anything from fish to vegetables!

Romesco
3 red bell peppers
5 tablespoons extra virgin olive oil
1 slice coarse-textured white bread
¼ cup blanched almonds
1½ cups peeled, seeded, chopped tomatoes, fresh or canned
1 clove garlic, minced
2 teaspoons sweet paprika
¼ teaspoon crushed red pepper flakes
4 tablespoons sherry vinegar
Salt and freshly ground black pepper

Shrimp
2 tablespoons extra virgin olive oil
30 large shrimp (about 1¼ pounds), peeled
1 clove garlic, minced
Flat-leaf parsley leaves as a garnish

Preheat the broiler.

Cut the bell peppers in half lengthwise and remove the stems, seeds, and ribs. Place them cut side down on a baking sheet. Broil the peppers until the entire skin is black, 6 to 10 minutes. Transfer the peppers to a plastic bag, close tightly, and let cool for 10 minutes. Using your fingers, peel off the skin. Cut the peppers into 1-inch dice.

Heat 1 tablespoon of the olive oil in a skillet over medium heat. Add the bread and fry it, turning occasionally, until golden on both sides. Transfer the bread to a food processor, leaving the oil in the skillet. In the same skillet, over medium heat, fry the almonds, stirring, until golden, 2 minutes. Add the almonds, tomatoes, garlic, paprika, and red pepper flakes to the processor and pulse several times. Combine the sherry vinegar and the remaining 4 tablespoons olive oil in a small pitcher. With the processor running, gradually add the olive oil mixture. Season with salt and pepper. Let sit 1 hour before using.

Prepare the shrimp: Warm the olive oil in a skillet over medium-high heat. Add the shrimp and cook for 1 minute. Add the garlic and continue to cook, stirring occasionally, until the shrimp are pink, almost firm to the touch, and curled, 2 to 3 minutes.

Arrange the shrimp on a platter and garnish with parsley. Place the *romesco* sauce in a small bowl and serve it on the side.                                                    Serves 6

Wine Suggestion: Merlot, Cabernet Sauvignon,
or amontillado sherry

# hot crispy beets "in their jackets" with lemon mint aïoli

I call these "in their jackets" because the beets are deep-fried in batter, producing a nice crispy coating. The batter is hot from the cayenne pepper and combines well with the sweetness of the beets. Serve the beets hot so that the lemon mint aïoli melts on them when dipped.

3 pounds beets, red and/or yellow

2 tablespoons extra virgin olive oil

Salt

1 recipe Lemon Mint Aïoli (recipe follows)

2¼ cups all-purpose flour

1 teaspoon salt

¼ teaspoon freshly ground black pepper

¼ teaspoon cayenne pepper

2 eggs

2 cups dry white wine

Mixture of olive oil and canola oil for deep-frying

6 lemon wedges as a garnish

Spearmint sprigs as a garnish

Preheat the oven to 400°F.

Wash the beets well and place them in a baking dish that's large enough to hold them in a single layer. Drizzle with the olive oil and sprinkle with salt. Roll the beets around to coat them with the oil. Cover with foil and bake until tender, 40 to 60 minutes.

In the meantime, prepare the Lemon Mint Aïoli.

When the beets are done, remove the foil and let them cool. When they are cool, slide off the skin with your fingers or with a paring knife. Cut the beets into ¼-inch-thick slices.

Stir the flour, salt, pepper, and cayenne together in a shallow bowl. In another

bowl, whisk together the eggs and wine. Slowly add the liquid to the flour mixture, whisking to obtain a smooth batter. Add the beets and stir to coat the slices with the batter.

Heat 2 to 3 inches of the oil mixture to 375°F in a deep heavy pan over medium-high heat. Using a slotted spoon, remove the beets from the batter and let drain. Fry them, in batches, in the hot oil until golden on each side and crisp, 3 minutes. Drain on paper towels.

Place a small bowl of the Lemon Mint Aïoli on a platter and surround it with the beets. Garnish with lemon wedges and mint sprigs. Serve immediately.          **Serves 8**

**Wine Suggestion: Bandol rosé**

## lemon mint aïoli

1 egg yolk

1 teaspoon Dijon mustard

½ cup olive oil

½ cup peanut, vegetable, corn, or safflower oil

2 to 3 cloves garlic, mashed with a mortar and pestle

Juice of 1 lemon

Salt and freshly ground black pepper

3 tablespoons chopped fresh spearmint

¾ teaspoon finely grated lemon zest

In a small bowl, whisk the egg yolk, mustard, and 1 tablespoon of the olive oil together until an emulsion is formed. In a measuring cup or small pitcher, combine the remaining olive oil and the peanut oil. Drop by drop, add the oil mixture to the emulsion, whisking constantly. Continue to do this in a fine steady stream, whisking, until all of the oil has been added. Do not add the oil too quickly, and be sure that the emulsion is homogeneous before adding more oil. Add the garlic, lemon juice, and salt and pepper to taste. Stir in the mint and lemon zest.

To thin the aïoli, add 1 to 3 tablespoons warm water to the mayonnaise in a thin stream, whisking constantly. Aïoli should be used the same day that it is made. Let it sit 30 minutes before serving.                                  **Makes about 1 cup**

*Note: The use of raw eggs carries the risk of salmonella poisoning. Dishes containing raw eggs should not be consumed by the very young, the very old, pregnant women, or anyone with a compromised immune system.*

# soups

spicy mussel stew with tomatoes and basil

green garlic and new potato soup

creamy fennel soup

tuscan winter white bean soup

barley and root vegetable soup

baked onion and bread soup

roasted butternut squash and carrot soup

farro and white bean soup

wild mushroom soup with blue cheese toasts

# the people at my table

**I've never met a person** who didn't like soup. With a loaf of bread, and maybe a glass of wine, it is meal enough. Soups are not a lot of work, are infinitely versatile, and are easily made ahead and rewarmed. Whether delicate first course or hearty main course, soups incorporate an amazing array of ingredients, flavors, and colors.

I love all the different textures of soup: compare Creamy Fennel Soup to Spring Soup of Favas, Sugar Snap Peas, and Asparagus. Isn't it great how substantial they all can be? Think of Spicy Mussel Stew with Tomatoes and Basil; it's a meal in its own right. There is a soup for every season. Can you imagine winter without something like Wild Mushroom Soup with Blue Cheese Toasts; spring without a fresh soup like Green Garlic and New Potato Soup; or summer without tomato soup—maybe Heirloom Tomato Bisque?

For me, cooking and eating are never about just getting through a meal. I think we have some obligation to nurture those at our table. Soup is the course that nourishes body and soul and warms the spirit.

# italian bread and tomato soup

The Italian name for this soup is *pappa al pomodoro,* literally "tomato mush." But don't be misled—this old-time recipe from Tuscany has great flavor and texture. It must be made at the height of summer, when the basil is fresh and sweet and the tomatoes are at their finest. And as they do in Tuscany, you must use stale coarse-textured bread.

¼ cup extra virgin olive oil

10 cloves garlic, thinly sliced

4 large very ripe red tomatoes, peeled, seeded, and diced (about 5 cups)

6 slices stale (2 to 3 days' old) coarse-textured country-style bread, cut ½-inch thick

3 cups chicken stock

2 cups water

Salt and freshly ground black pepper

1 teaspoon chopped fresh oregano

⅓ cup coarsely torn fresh basil (¼- to ½-inch pieces)

In a large soup pot, heat the olive oil over medium heat. Add the garlic and stir for 30 seconds. Add the tomatoes and bread, and cook until the bread falls apart, 5 to 10 minutes. Increase the heat to high, add the chicken stock, water, and salt and pepper to taste, and bring to a boil. Reduce the heat and simmer for 15 minutes, stirring occasionally. Remove from the heat, cover, and let sit for 5 minutes. Then stir in the oregano and basil, and season to taste with salt and pepper. (This soup can be made 1 day in advance and reheated.)

Ladle the hot soup into bowls and serve immediately.                    Serves 6

Wine Suggestion: Pinot Noir or Merlot

# roasted yellow pepper, corn, and tomato soup

Roasting the vegetables gives this soup a great smoky flavor. Be sure to make it at the height of summer, when corn is in season.

    4 yellow bell peppers
    3 ears of corn, in the husk
    4 ripe yellow tomatoes
    2 tablespoons extra virgin olive oil
    2 yellow onions, chopped
    6 cups chicken stock
    Kosher salt and freshly ground black pepper
    2 tablespoons snipped fresh chives

Preheat an outdoor grill.

Place the bell peppers, corn, and tomatoes on the rack and grill, turning occasionally, until the tomato skins are black and cracked, 4 to 5 minutes. Set the tomatoes aside to cool and continue grilling until the peppers are completely black and the corn husks are brown, another 2 to 3 minutes. Let the vegetables cool. (Alternatively, the peppers, corn, and tomatoes can be speared on a long-handled fork and charred over the burner of a gas stove.)

Peel the peppers. Cut them in half and remove the core and seeds. Coarsely chop. Husk the corn and remove the kernels from the cob. Core the tomatoes and coarsely chop. Place the peppers, corn, and tomatoes in a bowl and reserve.

In a large soup pot, warm the olive oil over medium heat. Add the onions and cook until soft, 7 minutes. Add the peppers, corn, and tomatoes and cook, stirring occasionally, for 3 minutes. Increase the heat to high, add the chicken stock, and bring to a boil. Reduce the heat to low and simmer until the tomatoes fall apart, 30 minutes. Let the soup cool for 20 minutes.

Puree the mixture, in several batches, in a blender until smooth, 2 to 3 minutes.

Strain through a fine-mesh strainer into a clean soup pot. Season to taste with salt and pepper, and bring back to a simmer.

Ladle the hot soup into bowls, and garnish each serving with 1 teaspoon of the chives. Serve immediately.

Serves 6

Wine Suggestion: Sauvignon Blanc

## grilling corn

Grilling corn gives it a slightly smoky flavor that adds a lot to a dish.

The simplest method is to leave the corn in its husk and set it on an outdoor grill or on a ridged cast-iron grill set on the stove. Grill it for 7 to 8 minutes, turning occasionally, until the husk is black and the kernels are beginning to turn a golden brown (just pull back a little of the husk to check).

# heirloom tomato bisque

It seems everyone has discovered the remarkable flavor and appearance of heirloom tomatoes, so you should be able to find them at your local farmer's market. My dictionary defines *heirloom* as "any treasured possession handed down from generation to generation." Well, I remember my grandmother growing heirloom tomatoes. I didn't realize she was so ahead of her time! She used them to make this American classic: a thick, rich soup of summer tomatoes with a dose of cream for sweetness. Use a blender, not a food processor, to puree the soup, to give it a velvety texture. You can also make it with yellow tomatoes, but you won't get the same depth of flavor.

1 tablespoon olive oil

1 red onion, chopped

8 large ripe red tomatoes, peeled, seeded, and chopped

4 cups chicken stock

1 teaspoon sugar

1 cup heavy cream

Salt and freshly ground black pepper

¼ cup chopped fresh mint

Heat the olive oil in a large soup pot over medium-high heat. Add the onions and cook, stirring occasionally, until soft, 7 minutes. Add the tomatoes, chicken stock, and sugar, and bring to a boil over high heat. Reduce the heat to medium-low and simmer until the mixture has reduced by one-fourth, 20 minutes. Allow to cool for 10 minutes.

Then puree the soup, in several batches, in a blender until smooth, 2 to 3 minutes per batch. Strain into a clean soup pot and bring to a simmer over medium heat. Remove from the heat and stir in the cream. Taste, and season with salt and pepper as needed. (This can be made up to 2 days in advance and reheated.)

Ladle the hot soup into bowls, garnish with the mint, and serve.          Serves 6

**Wine Suggestion: Sauvignon Blanc**

# summer vegetable soup

This soup of summer vegetables is inspired by the traditional *minestrone* of Liguria, Italy. In Provence, the French add a dollop of *pistou* or pesto and call it *soupe au pistou*. In both countries it is traditionally made with white beans, but I've substituted lentils in this version. In the height of summer, this soup is delicious served cold.

½ cup dry green or brown lentils

3 tablespoons extra virgin olive oil

1 small yellow onion, cut into ½-inch dice

1 small carrot, cut into ½-inch dice

2 cups peeled, seeded, chopped tomatoes, fresh or canned

4 cups chicken stock

3 cups water

¼ pound fresh green beans, trimmed and cut into ½-inch lengths

¼ pound dried fusilli pasta

2 ears of corn, kernels removed

½ bunch (4 to 6 ounces) Swiss chard, stems removed, cut into 1-inch pieces

2 tablespoons chopped fresh mint

Salt and freshly ground black pepper

½ cup grated Parmigiano-Reggiano cheese

Pick over the lentils and discard any stones or damaged lentils. Place the lentils in a large saucepan, cover with plenty of water, and simmer until lentils are tender, 15 to 20 minutes. Drain.

Heat the olive oil in a large soup pot over medium-low heat. Add the onions and carrots. Cook, stirring occasionally, until tender, 10 to 15 minutes. Add the tomatoes, chicken stock, and water. Cover and simmer for 30 minutes.

Fifteen minutes before serving, add the lentils, green beans, and pasta to the soup.

Simmer, covered, until the pasta is completely cooked, 8 to 10 minutes. Add the corn kernels, Swiss chard, and mint, and simmer until the Swiss chard wilts, 5 minutes. Season with salt and pepper.

Ladle the soup into bowls, sprinkle with Parmigiano, and serve immediately.

Serves 8

Wine Suggestion: Chardonnay or Pinot Noir

# the farmer's market

In the U.S., the supermarket has replaced the open-air marketplaces lined with farm stands and specialty shops that are the norm in the rest of the world. I am not knocking the convenience or selection that supermarkets provide, but there is some loss in freshness, in connection to the seasons and the farmers themselves.

Sometimes, it is okay to sacrifice a little convenience for freshness and flavor. That's why farmer's markets are growing in popularity. You meet the person who grew the food. You don't have to wonder which fruits are sweetest; they will tell you, and maybe give you a sample. The grapes still have the must on them, the zucchini are still dusty. No one has waxed the apples or picked the fruit early and let it ripen in transit. At the farmer's market the shelf life is short—get there early to get the best!

The best part of visiting the farmer's market is not spending the morning in the sun, surrounded by the sights, colors, and smells of ripe, ready-to-eat fruits and vegetables. Nor is it bringing your treasures home and cooking them. The best part is the look on your friends' and family's faces when they taste the full ripe flavors of food that is very fresh and ready, really ready, to be eaten.

# summer soup with herb-rolled pappardelle

This is an elegant soup that is great for entertaining. A mixture of herbs is placed between transparent layers of pappardelle, a wide flat noodle, creating a dramatic see-through effect. I like to make the pasta early and then simmer it with the summer vegetables and stock just before serving time.

> 1 cup all-purpose flour
>
> ⅛ teaspoon salt
>
> 1 egg
>
> 2 teaspoons water
>
> ¾ cup loosely packed mixture of herbs (flat-leaf parsley, sage, oregano, basil, mint, all stems removed)
>
> 9 cups chicken stock
>
> ½ cup sliced fresh green beans (¼-inch slices)
>
> 1 large carrot, cut into ¼-inch dice
>
> 1 green or yellow summer squash, halved, seeds removed, cut into ¼-inch dice
>
> ½ red bell pepper, seeds and membrane removed, cut into ¼-inch dice
>
> ½ cup grated Parmigiano-Reggiano cheese

In the bowl of a food processor, pulse together the flour and salt. Add the egg and water, and process until the dough forms a soft ball but is not sticky. (If it is sticky, add more flour, a tablespoon at a time, until it isn't.) Remove the dough from the processor and knead it on a very lightly floured surface until soft and smooth, 2 to 3 minutes. Wrap the dough in plastic wrap, and let it rest for at least 30 minutes, or up to 24 hours in the refrigerator.

Divide the dough into 3 pieces. With a pasta machine, roll one piece out to ⅛-inch thickness. Place the sheet of pasta flat on a lightly floured work surface. Scatter ¼ cup of the herb mixture over half the length of the sheet of pasta. Spray a light mist of water over the herbs. Fold the other half of the pasta over the herbs, and press the layers together. Continue to roll out the sheet of pasta until it is ¹⁄₁₆-inch thick. Using a scal-

loped pastry cutter, cut the pasta into 1-inch-wide strips. Toss with flour. Repeat with the remaining 2 pieces of pasta and ½ cup herbs. The dough can be placed on a well-floured baking sheet and allowed to sit at room temperature for several hours, or covered with a kitchen towel in the refrigerator overnight.

Warm the chicken stock in a large soup pot over medium-high heat. Add the green beans, carrots, summer squash, and bell pepper, and simmer until the vegetables are almost tender, 2 to 3 minutes. Add the pappardelle and continue to simmer until the pasta is tender, 1 to 2 minutes.

Ladle the hot soup into bowls, garnish with the Parmigiano, and serve.

Serves 6 to 8

Wine Suggestion: Chardonnay or Pinot Grigio

# farmer's market squash soup with basil

Don't you love going to your local farmer's market? I do. Whenever I have the chance, I get my big canvas bag and head down to our local market to see what looks really good. One day, I saw all kinds of different squash and I was inspired to make this soup. If I see any squash blossoms, I like to just chop them and throw them in the soup at the last minute. They impart a nice peppery flavor.

3 tablespoons extra virgin olive oil

1 yellow onion, cut into ½-inch dice

2 cloves garlic, thinly sliced

2 zucchini (about ¾ pound), cut into ½-inch dice

2 yellow summer squash (about ½ pound), cut into ½-inch dice

3 pattypan squash (about ½ pound), cut into ½-inch dice

5 cups chicken stock

1 cup water

¼ cup slivered fresh basil

1 teaspoon chopped fresh oregano

Salt and freshly ground black pepper

¾ cup grated Parmigiano-Reggiano cheese

Warm the olive oil in a large soup pot over medium heat. Add the onions and cook, stirring occasionally, until soft, 7 minutes. Add the garlic, and stir constantly for 30 seconds. Add the zucchini, yellow squash, pattypan squash, chicken stock, and water. Increase the heat to high and bring to a boil. Immediately reduce the heat to low and simmer until the squash is tender, 5 minutes. Add the basil and oregano, and simmer for 1 minute. Season with salt and pepper.

Ladle the hot soup into bowls, sprinkle with the Parmigiano, and serve.

Serves 6

Wine Suggestion: Sauvignon Blanc

# chilled cucumber yogurt soup with pita crisps

Cucumbers are so cool and crispy that they make a refreshing component in a chilled summer soup. When choosing cucumbers, avoid the waxed variety sold in grocery stores year-round. Instead pick the long, thin-skinned English variety sealed in plastic wrap. They have a superior flavor and fewer seeds. This soup is inspired by *tzatziki,* a Greek yogurt, garlic, and cucumber dip or puree that is usually served before the meal. I added milk to the combination to make this refreshing soup, which satisfies one's desire for the flavors of Mediterranean herbs and garlic. Serve it on a fiery hot day.

### Pita crisps
3 pita breads (8-inch diameter)

3 tablespoons extra virgin olive oil

Kosher salt

### Soup
3 cups plain full-fat yogurt, drained in a cheesecloth- or paper-towel-lined strainer
   for 4 hours

1 large cucumber, peeled, seeded, and coarsely grated

2 cloves garlic, minced

2 tablespoons extra virgin olive oil

3 tablespoons chopped fresh mint

3 tablespoons chopped fresh dill

2 cups cold milk

3 tablespoons white wine vinegar or fresh lemon juice

Salt and freshly ground black pepper

Preheat the oven to 375°F.

    Separate each pita bread into 2 rounds. Cut each round into 8 wedges, and place them in a single layer on a baking sheet. Drizzle with the olive oil and sprinkle with salt. Toss together. Bake the pita wedges in the oven until crisp and light golden, 10 to 12 minutes. Remove from the oven and allow to cool.

Prepare the soup: Discard any water that has drained from the yogurt. Combine the drained yogurt, cucumber, garlic, olive oil, 2 tablespoons of the mint, the dill, and the milk. Mix well. Add the vinegar, and salt and pepper to taste. Chill until ice cold, 1 hour.

Ladle the chilled soup into bowls, and garnish each serving with a mound of pita crisps in the center. Sprinkle with the remaining 1 tablespoon mint, and serve.

**Serves 6**

**Wine Suggestion: Sauvignon Blanc**

# spring soup of favas, sugar snap peas, and asparagus

In Italy, if you go out for dinner but you're not really hungry, you order *pasta en brodo*, "pasta in broth." What I've done here is to add some wonderful springtime vegetables to the broth—fava beans, sugar snap peas, and asparagus—all of which come into season at the same time. You could also add English peas, if you like.

> 1 pound fresh fava beans in the pod, shelled
>
> ½ pound sugar snap peas
>
> ½ pound asparagus, ends removed
>
> 9 cups chicken stock
>
> 6 ounces dried farfalle (bow-tie) pasta
>
> 1 tablespoon fresh lemon juice
>
> Salt and freshly ground black pepper
>
> ½ cup grated Parmigiano-Reggiano cheese

Bring a pot three-fourths full of water to a boil. Add the fava beans and simmer for 20 seconds. Drain and let cool. Split open the skin of each bean along its edge, and slip the bean from the skin. Discard the skins.

Remove the ends and strings from the sugar snap peas. Cut the snap peas on the diagonal into 1-inch pieces. Reserve.

Cut the asparagus into 1-inch lengths and reserve.

In a large pot, bring the chicken stock to a boil. Add the farfalle and cook until al dente, 8 to 10 minutes. Add the fava beans, sugar snap peas, asparagus, and lemon juice and simmer for 2 minutes. Season to taste with salt and pepper.

Ladle the soup into bowls and serve immediately. Pass the Parmigiano at the table.

Serves 6

Wine Suggestion: Pinot Grigio, Bandol rosé, or Sauvignon Blanc

# spicy mussel stew with tomatoes and basil

This delicious soup, sweet with basil and tomatoes, was inspired by a dish I had in a village restaurant in Liguria. It's a thick soup that borders on being a stew and incorporates all of the flavors I love, including my trinity of revered ingredients—garlic, tomatoes, and olive oil. It doesn't take long to make. You can substitute clams for the mussels.

6 tablespoons extra virgin olive oil

1 yellow onion, chopped

4 cloves garlic, thinly sliced

3 cups peeled, seeded, chopped tomatoes, fresh or canned

¼ teaspoon crushed red pepper flakes

1 cup water

Salt and freshly ground black pepper

4 pounds mussels, scrubbed, beards removed

1 cup dry white wine

3 tablespoons capers, rinsed

½ cup torn fresh basil

2 teaspoons chopped fresh flat-leaf parsley

6 slices coarse-textured bread, toasted or grilled

2 cloves garlic

Warm 2 tablespoons of the olive oil in a large, heavy soup pot over medium heat. Add the onions and cook until soft, 7 minutes. Add the garlic and cook, stirring, for 30 seconds. Increase the heat to high, and add the tomatoes, red pepper flakes, and water. Bring to a boil. Reduce the heat to low, season with salt and pepper, and simmer for 20 minutes.

In the meantime, warm 2 tablespoons of the olive oil in a large sauté pan over medium-high heat. Add the mussels, cover, and cook, shaking the pan frequently, until they open, 3 to 5 minutes. As they open, remove the mussels with tongs. When all of the mussels are open, increase the heat to high. Immediately add the wine and cook

3 to 5 minutes, until reduced by half. Remove the pan from the heat. Remove half of the mussels from the shells. Add the mussels (shelled and unshelled), reduced white wine, tomato mixture, capers, basil, and parsley. Season with salt and pepper. Bring to a simmer over medium heat before serving.

Rub the toast with the garlic cloves, and brush with the remaining 2 tablespoons olive oil. Ladle the soup into bowls and garnish with the toast.

Serves 6

**Wine Suggestion: Chardonnay**

# green garlic and new potato soup

Green garlic is nothing but immature garlic, picked before it forms cloves and their papery sheaths. It resembles baby leeks or scallions, with its long green tops and white bulb, sometimes streaked with light pink. Look for green garlic at your local farmer's market in early spring. If you can't find it, substitute mature garlic—but use just half the amount because green garlic has a much milder flavor. Don't forget to season the soup with salt; otherwise the flavor will be boring.

1 tablespoon unsalted butter

24 young green garlic bulbs (about ½ pound), ½- to 1-inch diameter at the root end

8 cups chicken stock

1½ pounds new red potatoes, quartered

¼ cup heavy cream

2 tablespoons white wine vinegar

Salt and freshly ground black pepper

Garnish

1 tablespoon extra virgin olive oil

8 to 10 scallions, thinly sliced

2 tablespoons chopped fresh flat-leaf parsley

Salt and freshly ground black pepper

Melt the butter in a soup pot over low heat. Add the garlic and ½ cup of the chicken stock, cover, and cook until the garlic is soft, 20 minutes. Add the potatoes and the remaining 7½ cups stock, increase the heat to high, and bring to a boil. Reduce the heat to low and simmer, covered, until the potatoes are soft, 20 minutes. Remove the pan from the heat and let cool for 20 minutes.

Puree the soup, in several batches, in a blender until very smooth, 3 to 4 minutes per batch. Strain it through a fine-mesh strainer into a clean soup pot. Add the cream and vinegar and mix well. Season to taste with salt and pepper, and bring back to a simmer.

For the garnish, heat the olive oil in a small saucepan over low heat. Add the scallions and stir constantly until soft, 1 minute. Add the parsley and stir together. Season to taste with salt and pepper.

Ladle the hot soup into bowls, and garnish with the scallion mixture. Serve immediately.

Serves 6

Wine Suggestion: Chardonnay

# creamy fennel soup

When I was a kid, I never ate black licorice and didn't even really like the red. But when I tasted fresh fennel as an adult, I loved it! It has that delicious, delicate flavor of licorice, which is a great match for the garlic in this soup. I like to cook the croutons in a little butter flavored with finely ground fennel seeds and then rub them with garlic.

5 bulbs fennel with stalks and feathery green tops (2½ to 3 pounds)
2 tablespoons extra virgin olive oil
1 yellow onion, coarsely chopped
1 clove garlic, minced
8 cups chicken stock
½ cup heavy cream
Salt and freshly ground black pepper
2 tablespoons unsalted butter
⅛ teaspoon finely ground fennel seeds
18 thin slices baguette
1 clove garlic

Remove the greens from the fennel stalks, chop them, and set aside to use as a garnish. Cut the fennel bulbs and stalks into coarse pieces.

Heat the olive oil in a soup pot over medium heat. Add the onions and cook until soft, 7 minutes. Add the garlic and continue to cook, stirring constantly, for 30 seconds. Increase the heat to high. Add the chopped fennel and the chicken stock, and bring to a boil. Reduce to a simmer and cook until the fennel is very tender, 15 minutes. Allow to cool slightly.

Puree the soup, in batches, in a blender until very smooth. Strain through a fine-mesh strainer into a clean soup pot. Add the cream, and season with salt and pepper.

Melt the butter in a large frying pan over medium heat. Add the ground fennel seeds and stir for 30 seconds. Add the baguette slices in a single layer, and cook, turning once, until golden on both sides, 2 to 3 minutes total. Season with salt to taste. Remove the baguette slices from the pan and rub each piece lightly on one side with the clove of garlic.

Warm the soup over medium heat. Ladle it into bowls, and place a few baguette slices on top. Garnish with the reserved fennel greens,  and serve immediately.

**Serves 6**

**Wine Suggestion: Chardonnay**

# tuscan winter white bean soup

I'm cheating a little bit here. This hearty Tuscan soup is called *ribollita,* which means "reboiled"—a reference to the fact that it is cooked once, cooled, and then reheated. (I just cook it once.) It's traditionally made with beans, vegetables, bread, and black cabbage, and is supposed to be thick enough to eat with a fork. I substitute Savoy cabbage because black cabbage is rarely available in the United States. And I leave out the bread; if you want your soup thicker, add some stale coarse-textured bread with the vegetables. If you'd like, drizzle some fruity extra virgin olive oil on to the top of the soup just before serving.

½ cup dried cannellini beans

4 tablespoons extra virgin olive oil

½ pound pancetta, cut into ¼-inch dice

½ stalk celery, cut into ¼-inch dice

2 small carrots, cut into ½-inch dice

½ head Savoy cabbage, cut into 1-inch dice

2 leeks, cut into ½-inch dice

2 red potatoes, unpeeled, cut into ½-inch dice

1 yellow onion, cut into ¼-inch dice

1 tablespoon tomato paste

3 cups chicken stock

3 cups water

Salt and freshly ground black pepper

Pick over the cannellini beans and discard any stones or damaged beans. Place the beans in a large bowl, cover with plenty of cold water, and soak for 4 hours. Drain the beans and place them in a large saucepan.

Cover with plenty of water and simmer until they are tender and the skins are just beginning to crack, 45 to 60 minutes. Drain the beans and reserve the cooking liquid. Place half of the beans in a blender, add ½ cup reserved cooking liquid, and puree until smooth. Reserve the puree and the remaining beans.

Heat the olive oil in a soup pot over medium heat. Add the pancetta and cook, stirring occasionally, until it is light golden, 10 minutes. Drain off and discard all but 2 tablespoons of the fat in the pot. Add the celery, carrots, cabbage, leeks, potatoes, onions, tomato paste, chicken stock, and 3 cups water. Bring to a boil. Reduce the heat and simmer until the vegetables are very soft, 45 minutes.

Add the whole cannellini beans and the bean puree, and simmer uncovered for 5 minutes. Season with salt and pepper. Serve immediately.                **Serves 6**

**Wine Suggestion: Chianti**

# barley and root vegetable soup

This hearty soup was inspired by the ones my mother loved to make for the family during the cold New England winters. Sometimes she would add dried lentils, black beans, or kidney beans to make a really substantial, heartwarming, stick-to-your-ribs soup. I've used barley in this one, and lots of root vegetables. You could also add turnips or other vegetables, such as butternut or acorn squash. This soup needs nothing more than a crusty roll, a salad, and a glass of wine to make a wonderful meal.

12 cups chicken or vegetable stock

½ cup pearl barley

2 carrots (about 6 ounces), cut into ¾-inch dice

2 parsnips (about 6 ounces), cut into ¾-inch dice

2 potatoes (about ¾ pound), cut into ¾-inch dice

1 cup broccoli florets, about ¼ pound, cut into ¾-inch pieces

1 rutabaga (about ½ pound), cut into ¾-inch pieces

1 teaspoon chopped fresh thyme

1 teaspoon chopped fresh oregano

Salt and freshly ground black pepper

1 tablespoon chopped fresh flat-leaf parsley

Bring the stock to a boil in a large soup pot over high heat. Add the barley, reduce the heat to medium-low, cover, and simmer until it is almost tender, 15 to 20 minutes.

Increase the heat to medium-high. Add the carrots, parsnips, potatoes, broccoli, rutabaga, thyme, and oregano. Simmer until the vegetables are tender, 10 minutes. Season with salt and pepper.

Ladle the hot soup into bowls, garnish with the chopped parsley, and serve.

Serves 6

Wine Suggestion: Chardonnay or Pinot Noir

# pinot noir

Some people say that if they had one wine to drink for the rest of their life, it would be Pinot Noir. Of all wines, in my estimation, it is the most food-friendly. But it is also one of the most difficult to find at a good price.

Pinot Noir, the grape variety responsible for all red burgundies, has its roots in Burgundy, where it has been grown for hundreds of years, perhaps as early as the 4th century A.D. This very old vine variety is prone to mutate (Pinot Blanc, Pinot Gris, Pinot Meunier) and to degenerate (there are forty-six Pinot Noir clones within France).

A superior and versatile wine, it is not surprising that the Pinot Noir vine has been transplanted to virtually every corner of the globe where wine is made, with the exception of the hottest areas. It likes a cool climate, which is why Carneros, in the California wine country, and Burgundy produce such remarkable Pinot Noir.

It requires considerable skill on the part of the vine grower and winemaker, though. If Pinot Noir could be said to have a common taste, it might be a sweet fruitiness (some say the classic flavor is of cherries and raspberries) and lower amounts of tannins and pigments than a Cabernet Sauvignon or a Syrah.

Pinot Noir is excellent with grilled or baked salmon or other seafood, with roasted duck or other game birds, and with a red meat dish like beef or lamb stew. You can see it is one of my particular favorites. I like it with almost everything!

# baked onion and bread soup

This hearty soup, called a *panade* in French, is really a cross between a soup and a gratin; that is, you make a gratin and then add broth to it. At Chez Panisse we used to make it in the winter, sometimes with butternut squash or potatoes.

⅓ cup olive oil

3 pounds onions, thinly sliced

Salt and freshly ground black pepper

¼ teaspoon dried thyme

6 slices rustic sourdough bread, cut ⅜-inch thick

2 cloves garlic

1 cup red Zinfandel wine

4 cups chicken stock

4 tablespoons grated Parmigiano-Reggiano cheese

Heat 3 tablespoons of the olive oil in a heavy flameproof casserole. Add the onions, salt and pepper to taste, and the thyme. Stir well to coat the onions. Cook over low heat, so the onions are sizzling a bit, stirring occasionally, for 1 hour, until golden and caramelized.

Meanwhile, preheat the oven to 375°F.

Brush the bread slices with the remaining olive oil, place them on a baking sheet, and bake them in the oven until they are lightly golden, about 15 to 20 minutes, turning them halfway through. Rub the toast with the garlic cloves and set aside. Leave the oven on.

Add the wine to the onions and cook over medium heat until reduced by one-fourth, 3 to 4 minutes. Add the chicken stock and season with salt and pepper to taste.

Break each slice of toasted bread into 3 or 4 large pieces, and layer half of them in an 8 x 12-inch baking dish. Using a slotted spoon, cover the bread with half of the onions, forming a thick layer. Set 3 cups of the onion broth aside. Ladle half of the remaining onion broth over the bread and onions, and sprinkle with 2 tablespoons of the Parmigiano. Repeat the layers of bread, onions, broth, and cheese.

Bake in the oven until most of the broth has been absorbed and the cheese has formed a golden layer, 45 minutes. (You may have to broil the top to make it crusty and golden.)

Keeping the layers intact, spoon the gratin into individual bowls. Quickly heat the reserved 3 cups broth, divide it among the bowls, and serve.                    Serves 6

**Wine Suggestion: Zinfandel**

# roasted butternut squash and carrot soup

This soup is perfect to serve when the weather begins to chill; its color and flavors just seem to belong to autumn. Toasting the spices first brings out all their flavor, and roasting the squash in the oven accentuates its natural sweetness. You'll be amazed at the depth of flavor.

1 butternut squash (1½ to 2 pounds)

3 tablespoons olive oil

1 large yellow onion, chopped

1½ teaspoons sweet paprika

1½ teaspoons ground cumin

1 teaspoon turmeric

1½ teaspoons ground coriander

4 large carrots, coarsely chopped

1 teaspoon sugar

3 cups chicken stock

3 cups water

Salt and freshly ground black pepper

½ cup plain yogurt

3 tablespoons chopped fresh cilantro

Preheat the oven to 375°F.

Cut the squash in half from top to bottom and place it, cut side down, on a lightly oiled baking sheet. Bake until the squash can be easily pierced with a knife, 50 to 60 minutes. Allow it to cool slightly. With a spoon, remove and discard the seeds. Scrape the pulp from the skin. Discard the skin.

Warm the olive oil in a soup pot over medium heat. Add the onions and cook until soft, 7 minutes. Add the paprika, cumin, turmeric, and coriander and continue to cook, stirring, for 2 minutes. Add the squash, carrots, sugar, chicken stock, water, ½ teaspoon salt, and ¼ teaspoon pepper. Bring to a boil, reduce the heat to low, and simmer, uncovered, until the carrots are soft, 20 to 25 minutes. Let cool for 15 minutes.

Puree the soup, in several batches, in a blender until it is very smooth, 3 minutes per batch. Strain it through a fine-mesh strainer back into the pot, and gently reheat. If the soup is too thick, add some water. Season with salt and pepper to taste.

Place the yogurt in a small bowl. Season it with salt and pepper, and stir well.

Ladle the hot soup into bowls, garnish with the cilantro and a drizzle of yogurt, and serve.

**Serves 6**

**Wine Suggestion: Sauvignon Blanc**

# farro and white bean soup

Farro is an ancient wheat grain that was cultivated by the Romans thousands of years ago. Today it's still a regular part of the diet in Tuscany and Umbria. The first time I had farro was in a bowl of autumn vegetable soup at a friend's 10th-century inn near Siena. The farro was crunchy and had a great nutty flavor. I like to drizzle fruity olive oil on the top just before serving this soup.

1½ cups (about 10 ounces) dried cannellini beans

1½ cups (about ½ pound) farro

2 tablespoons extra virgin olive oil

1 yellow onion, diced

1 large carrot, diced

1 stalk celery, diced

1 sprig fresh rosemary

2 cloves garlic, minced

1 cup peeled, seeded, chopped tomatoes, fresh or canned

4 cups chicken stock

Salt and freshly ground black pepper

Pick over the cannellini beans and discard any stones or damaged beans. Soak the beans overnight in a large bowl of water.

Place the farro in a bowl with plenty of water to cover. Let sit for 4 hours. Drain.

Drain the beans, place them in a saucepan, and add water to cover by 2 inches. Bring to a boil over high heat. Reduce the heat to low and simmer until tender, 45 to 60 minutes. Strain the beans, reserving the cooking liquid. In a blender, puree about half the beans with the cooking liquid to make a smooth paste. Reserve the puree and the remaining beans.

Warm the olive oil in a large soup pot over medium heat. Add the onions, carrots, celery, rosemary, and garlic. Cook, stirring occasionally, until the vegetables are soft, 10 to 12 minutes. Add the farro, whole cannellini beans, bean puree, tomatoes, and chicken stock. Bring to a boil. Reduce the heat to low, and simmer until the farro is tender and the soup is thick, 30 to 40 minutes. Season to taste with salt and pepper.

Ladle the hot soup into bowls and serve immediately. **Serves 8**

**Wine Suggestion: Sangiovese or Pinot Noir**

# wild mushroom soup with blue cheese toasts

Winter in the wine country means cold, rainy days—perfect for this soup. The flavor of wild mushrooms goes well with the blue cheese. (If you like this soup, try the Wild Mushroom and Blue Cheese Crostini in *Weir Cooking,* the book from my first show.) I like to use porcini, hedgehog, chanterelle, or morel mushrooms. If they aren't available, you can substitute fresh button mushrooms.

3 tablespoons unsalted butter

1 yellow onion, chopped

1 pound button mushrooms, coarsely chopped

1 ounce dried porcini mushrooms

6 cups chicken stock

4 cups water

½ pound fresh wild mushrooms, thinly sliced

Salt and freshly ground black pepper

½ cup heavy cream

1 tablespoon fresh lemon juice

Toasts

2 ounces blue cheese (Roquefort, Stilton, Gorgonzola), room temperature

Salt and freshly ground black pepper

6 slices baguette, cut ½-inch thick, toasted

2 tablespoons chopped fresh flat-leaf parsley

In a large soup pot over medium-high heat, melt 2 tablespoons of the butter. Add the onions and cook, stirring occasionally, until soft, 7 minutes. Increase the heat to high, and add the button mushrooms, porcini mushrooms, chicken stock, and water. Bring to a boil. Reduce the heat to medium-low and simmer, uncovered, until the mushrooms are tender, 30 minutes. Let cool for 15 minutes.

While the mixture is cooling, melt the remaining 1 tablespoon butter in a frying pan over medium-high heat. Add the sliced wild mushrooms and cook, stirring occasionally, until they are soft and the mushroom liquid has evaporated, 6 to 10 minutes. Season with salt and pepper. Remove from the pan and reserve.

In a blender, puree the cooled soup, in batches, until very smooth, 3 to 4 minutes per batch. Strain through a fine-mesh strainer into a clean soup pot. Add the cream and the sautéed wild mushrooms, and stir well to combine. Season with the lemon juice, and with salt and pepper to taste.

Preheat the broiler.

In a small bowl, mash the blue cheese until soft. Season it with salt and pepper to taste. Spread the cheese onto the toasted baguette slices. Place on a baking sheet and broil until the cheese is bubbling around the edges. Remove from the broiler and sprinkle with the parsley.

Bring the soup back to a simmer, and ladle the hot soup into bowls. Float a blue cheese toast in the center of each bowl, and serve immediately.          **Serves 6**

**Wine Suggestion: Pinot Noir**

# salads

stone fruit summer salad

melon, grape, fennel, and fig salad

summer salad of seared tuna, shell beans, and tomatoes

tartine salad with goat cheese and roasted tomato tapenade

grilled corn and arugula salad with shaved parmigiano

greek summer vegetable salad

tuscan bread salad with tomatoes and basil

fattoush

turkish olive and bread salad

chopped salad

arugula salad with bosc pears, stilton, and verjus

slow-roasted beet salad with parsley, celery, and fennel

true blue salad

romaine salad with oranges, walnuts, and manchego

layered salad of bulgur, fennel, pine nuts, dill, and mint

salad of pomegranates, grapes, apples, pears, and pecans with
frisée

warm frisée salad with pancetta-wrapped endive

sugar snap pea and mint salad with prosciutto

smoked trout and winter citrus salad

tuna niçoise

## season to season

**When I design a menu,** I begin by considering what is in season. This isn't to say that I never open a can of tomatoes in June. But using seasonal ingredients is a starting point for a process that has at its end the vivid flavor and color that the freshest foods provide.

With salads, this is a simple matter, especially in the summer. Farmer's markets, roadside stands, your own garden—all are full of vegetables and fruits that need only the smallest effort to bring out their flavor. A splash of balsamic vinegar or fennel oil, some fresh herbs, a little time on the grill. How about a slow-roasted beet salad with parsley, celery, and fennel? Or a salad of grilled corn and arugula? In the winter, when the temptation is great to pick up that wilty head of lettuce or that rock-hard pink tomato, I love to make a salad of in-season vegetables, or maybe one of winter citrus fruits and smoked trout.

When you begin to think and cook seasonally, you begin to immerse yourself in the cycles of life and are rewarded by the best flavor and texture each ingredient offers at its peak. When you can connect more with where our food comes from, you have the added joy of anticipating and then enjoying the short season of your favorite fruits and vegetables, knowing that it will be another year until you are so moved again.

# stone fruit summer salad

My friend Laurence Jossel, of Chez Nous in San Francisco, inspired this wine-friendly summer salad of stone fruits. Serve the salad with a glass of the same wine used in the dressing. This is a great way to get around the acidity of the vinaigrette when you want to pair wine with your salad. Or of course a Sauvignon Blanc will also work!

1 cup fruity Gewürztraminer wine

1 tablespoon white wine vinegar

1 tablespoon *verjus* (optional; see page 147)

1 tablespoon hazelnut or walnut oil

3 tablespoons extra virgin olive oil

Salt and freshly ground black pepper

⅓ cup almonds, whole or very coarsely chopped

1 ripe peach

1 ripe nectarine

1 ripe plum

1 ripe apricot

½ cup pitted ripe cherries

8 cups mixed salad greens

Place the wine in a saucepan and reduce over high heat until only 2 tablespoons remain, 2 to 4 minutes. Pour the reduced wine into a small bowl. Add the vinegar, *verjus*, hazelnut oil, and olive oil. Whisk together. Season with salt and pepper to taste.

Meanwhile, preheat the oven to 350°F.

Place the almonds on a baking sheet and toast in the oven until golden, 5 to 7 minutes. Let cool.

Just before serving, cut the peach, nectarine, plum, and apricot into ⅜-inch wedges. Toss the salad greens with the fruit, almonds, and vinaigrette. Serve immediately.

Serves 6

Wine Suggestion: Gewürztraminer

# melon, grape, fennel, and fig salad

I'm so lucky to have such great chef friends. This beautiful first-course summer salad was inspired by one created by my closest chef friend, Gary Danko, who has a marvelous restaurant in San Francisco. It utilizes a selection of sweet summer fruits topped off with shaved fennel and a slice of salty prosciutto. The dressing consists simply of a fennel-infused oil—no vinegar.

2 bunches frisée, about 8 to 10 ounces, stem ends removed, leaves separated

1 bulb fennel, thinly sliced

3 tablespoons Fennel Oil (recipe follows)

Salt and freshly ground black pepper

½ small melon (honeydew, Crenshaw, casaba, cantaloupe), thinly sliced

2 cups small grapes (if large, cut in half)

9 fresh figs, cut in half

6 thin slices prosciutto or Serrano ham, cut in half lengthwise

Place the frisée and fennel in a bowl. Add the Fennel Oil, season with salt and pepper, and toss together.

Arrange a few slices of melon on each salad plate. Distribute the grapes on the plates. Top the melon and grapes with the frisée mixture. Place the figs on top of the greens, and drape 2 slices of the prosciutto over the figs. Serve.          Serves 6

Wine Suggestion: Riesling

## fennel oil

1 cup extra virgin olive oil
3 tablespoons fennel seeds

Heat a dry frying pan over medium heat. Add the fennel seeds and cook, shaking the pan constantly, for 15 to 30 seconds, until fragrant. Do not allow them to turn brown.

Grind the fennel seeds in a clean coffee or spice grinder, or with a mortar and pestle, until coarsely ground.

Combine the olive oil and ground fennel seeds in a jar, and shake. Let sit at room temperature for 7 days.

After 7 days, strain. Keeps up to 6 months.                    **Makes 1 cup**

# summer salad of seared tuna, shell beans, and tomatoes

Although the season is short for fresh shell beans, summer is the time to find them. Because I love them so much, I was inspired to make this salad. It pairs shell beans and fresh grilled tuna that is served warm, with a garlic mayonnaise that melts on top.

1 recipe Aïoli (recipe follows)

2 to 3 tablespoons warm water

1½ cups shelled fresh shell beans (flageolets, black-eyed peas, cranberry beans, limas, cannellini, or a combination)

5 tablespoons red wine vinegar

5 tablespoons extra virgin olive oil

Salt and freshly ground black pepper

¾ pound fresh green beans

¾ pound fresh yellow (wax) beans

1¾ pounds fresh tuna steak

½ pound assorted cherry tomatoes (red, yellow, orange, pear-shaped, grape-shaped)

20 fresh basil leaves

Whisk the Aïoli with enough of the warm water to make a barely fluid sauce. Set it aside.

Heat an outdoor grill or an indoor ridged cast-iron grill.

Bring a pot of water to a boil over medium-high heat. Add the shell beans and cook until tender, 20 to 25 minutes. Drain, place in a large bowl, and toss with 4 tablespoons of the vinegar and all of the olive oil. Season with salt and pepper.

Bring another pot of salted water to a boil over medium-high heat. Add the green and yellow beans, and cook until tender but still slightly crisp, 4 to 7 minutes. Drain. Add to the shell beans and toss together.

Oil the tuna with a pastry brush, and grill it until golden and seared on one side, 3 to 4 minutes. Turn the tuna, season with salt and pepper, and continue to grill until it is slightly pink in the center, 3 to 5 minutes. Remove from the grill and reserve.

Halve the cherry tomatoes, place them in a bowl, and toss with the remaining 1 tablespoon vinegar. Season with salt and pepper, and toss together.

To serve, place the beans on a platter. Break the tuna into 1½-inch pieces and arrange them on top of the beans. Top with the tomatoes and a spoonful of the Aïoli. Garnish with the basil, and serve immediately with the remaining Aïoli on the side.

Serves 6

Wine Suggestion: Bandol rosé or Grenache rosé

## aïoli

This garlicky mayonnaise is delicious on vegetables and fish too.

> ½ cup olive oil (not extra virgin)
> ½ cup peanut, vegetable, corn, or safflower oil
> 1 egg yolk
> 1 teaspoon Dijon mustard
> 2 to 3 cloves garlic, minced or mashed with a mortar and pestle
> Juice of 1 lemon
> Salt and freshly ground black pepper

Combine the olive oil and the peanut oil in a liquid measuring cup or small pitcher.

In a small bowl, whisk the egg yolk, mustard, and 1 tablespoon of the combined oil together until an emulsion is formed. Add the remaining oil to the emulsion drop by drop, whisking constantly. Continue to do this in a fine steady stream, whisking, until all of the oil has been added. Do not add the oil too quickly, and be sure that the emulsion is homogeneous before adding more oil. Add the garlic and lemon juice and season with salt and pepper to taste.

This mayonnaise can be made 7 to 10 days in advance as long as the garlic isn't added until the day of serving.

Makes about 1 cup

*Note: Raw eggs carry the risk of salmonella poisoning. Dishes containing raw eggs should not be consumed by the very young, the very old, pregnant women, or anyone with a compromised immune system.*

# tartine salad with goat cheese and roasted tomato tapenade

A *tartine* is an open-face sandwich, currently much in vogue in France and in the U.S. Like Italian *crostini, tartines* can be made with any sort of topping—goat cheese, smoked salmon, tomatoes. These are made with *tapenade,* the traditional olive, caper, and anchovy paste from the south of France, to which I've added oven-roasted or sun-dried tomatoes. It balances really well with the goat cheese. To turn a sandwich into a salad, I simply toss in a few salad greens. It makes a terrific main course for an *al fresco* lunch.

**Roasted Tomato Tapenade:**

3 anchovy fillets

½ cup brine-cured pitted black olives (Niçoise or Kalamata)

2 cloves garlic, minced

3 tablespoons capers, rinsed and chopped

¼ teaspoon grated lemon zest

½ teaspoon *herbes de Provence*

2 tablespoons fresh lemon juice

1 cup finely chopped oven-roasted tomatoes (see page 134)

Salt and freshly ground black pepper

6 large slices rustic coarse-textured bread

1 clove garlic

6 ounces (about 1¼ cups) fresh goat cheese, room temperature

1 tablespoon red wine vinegar

3 tablespoons extra virgin olive oil

Salt and freshly ground black pepper

3 cups tender young salad greens

Prepare the tapenade:

Soak the anchovies in cold water for 10 minutes. Then pat them dry and mash them. Place the anchovies, olives, garlic, capers, lemon zest, and *herbes de Provence* in a food processor and pulse a few times to form a rough paste. Add the lemon juice and the tomatoes. Pulse 2 times. Season with salt and pepper to taste.

Toast the bread or grill it on an outdoor grill. Rub one side of the toast with the

# oven-roasted tomatoes

When it's the height of summer and you find yourself with more fresh tomatoes than you can use, one of the best things you can do is to preserve them by oven-drying. It's a simple process and brings out a lot of sweetness. I also like to use this technique when I just want that special flavor it imparts.

> 3 pounds plum tomatoes, cored, cut in half lengthwise
> 1 tablespoon kosher salt

Place the tomatoes, cut side up, on a baking sheet and sprinkle with the kosher salt. Let sit for 1 hour.

Preheat the oven to 250°F.

Bake the tomatoes until they are almost dry, yet still slightly soft and plump, 5 to 6 hours.

If not used right away, the tomatoes can be stored in self-seal plastic bags in the freezer for 2 to 3 months, or covered completely with olive oil in a glass jar and stored in the refrigerator for up to 10 days.

Makes 2 to 2¼ cups

garlic clove. Cut the bread in half diagonally. Spread the goat cheese evenly over the toasts, and then spread the tomato tapenade over the goat cheese.

In a small bowl, whisk together the vinegar and olive oil. Season with salt and pepper to taste.

Place 2 pieces of toast on each plate, overlapping slightly. Toss the salad greens with the vinaigrette. Pile the salad greens on top of the bread. Serve immediately.

Serves 6

Wine Suggestion: Sauvignon Blanc

# grilled corn and arugula salad with shaved parmigiano

When I compose a salad, or any dish for that matter, I try to think about blending sweet, salty, sour, and bitter tastes. This simple salad is a good example: there is the sweetness of the corn, the saltiness of the Parmigiano and the olives, the sour flavor of the lemon, and the bitterness and pepperiness from the arugula.

3 ears of corn, in the husk

½ clove garlic, chopped

1 tablespoon fresh lemon juice

¼ cup extra virgin olive oil

Salt and freshly ground black pepper

3 bunches arugula, stems removed (about 8 cups)

¾ cup oil-cured black olives

3-ounce chunk Parmigiano-Reggiano cheese

Preheat an outdoor charcoal grill or an indoor ridged cast-iron grill.

If you are using an outdoor grill, place the corn on the rack, 4 inches from the heat source, and grill, turning occasionally, until the husks are black and the kernels are light golden (pull back a little of the husk to check), 7 to 8 minutes. Remove the corn from the grill and let it cool. If you are using a ridged grill, place the corn on the grill and cook, turning occasionally, until the husks are black and the kernels are light golden, 9 to 10 minutes. Remove the husks and discard.

Cut the kernels from the cobs and reserve.

In a small bowl, whisk together the garlic, lemon juice, and olive oil. Season with salt and pepper to taste.

Toss the arugula, olives, and corn with the vinaigrette. Distribute among the serving plates, and shave the Parmigiano over the top. Serve immediately.          **Serves 6**

**Wine Suggestion: Sauvignon Blanc or Pinot Noir**

# my grandfather's farmstand

Among the pleasures of a New England childhood are the rustic farmstands that dot the country roads from late summer and through the fall, selling local produce. A hand-written sign proclaims "FRESHLY PICKED" and may refer to just a few boxes of apples or to a bounty of corn, squash, cucumbers, pumpkins, peaches, and pears. Even home gardeners set up shop along the roadside to market their harvest.

My grandparents were no different. Their farmstand burst with freshly picked fruits and vegetables. As a child, I loved to visit them there, pick an apple from one of the shelves, and eat it in the afternoon sun.

But what I remember most is the day my grandfather would pick the first corn of the season and bring a large bushel of it home—not to be sold, but to be eaten by all of us. My grandmother would have the water boiling as he came into the kitchen, his arms loaded. I'd watch him sit in a chair, lean over a paper bag, and husk the corn, dropping the husks and silk directly into the bag. He carefully piled up the corn, as if it were gold bullion.

My grandmother would add a fistful of salt to the water and then, one by one, drop the ears of corn into the water. After about four or five minutes, out they'd come. She would set a big platter of corn in the center of the table and we would make a meal of just fresh corn and homemade butter. My grandmother's butter was saltier than most, and this was the only time she'd let us run the corn along the butter, making a groove in it that perfectly matched the kernels of corn.

# greek summer vegetable salad

I used to wonder why this salad is made with green tomatoes in Greece, but one taste and the answer was clear: In Greece, green tomatoes are sweet, juicy, and delicious, nothing like their counterpart in this country. If you want this salad to taste its best, start with the freshest height-of-the-summer vegetables and a good fruity extra virgin olive oil.

3 large ripe red tomatoes (about 2 pounds), coarsely cut into 1- to 1½-inch pieces

1 small red onion, cut into 1-inch dice

1 red bell pepper, coarsely cut into 1-inch pieces

1 English (hothouse) cucumber, unpeeled, cut into 1-inch pieces

6 tablespoons extra virgin olive oil

3 tablespoons red wine vinegar

Salt and freshly ground black pepper

¾ pound feta cheese, about 2¼ cups

1 cup Kalamata olives

1½ teaspoons dried Greek oregano

Place the tomatoes, onions, bell peppers, and cucumbers on a serving platter.

In a bowl, whisk together the olive oil and vinegar. Season with salt and pepper to taste. Pour the vinaigrette over the vegetables.

Crumble the feta over the salad, sprinkle the olives and oregano over the top, and serve immediately.

Serves 8

Wine Suggestion: Sauvignon Blanc or Pinot Noir

## sauvignon blanc

Sauvignon Blanc is one of my favorite wines, and in my estimation, it's also one of the most food-friendly of all whites.

The vine variety responsible for some of the world's best dry white wines, Sauvignon Blanc is found in its purest form in the Loire Valley, in the vineyards of Sancerre and Pouilly-Fumé. But it is grown elsewhere, both in and out of France, and has been very successful in California, where Robert Mondavi renamed it Fumé Blanc to reflect its slightly smoky flavor (*fumé* means "smoked"). It is also an ingredient in the best whites of Bordeaux.

The flavor of Sauvignon Blanc is classically refreshing, zesty, herbaceous, smoky, with a citrus acidity, but not oaky. Some think its aroma is similar to Cabernet Sauvignon. In fact, it was recently established that Sauvignon Blanc and Cabernet Franc are parents to Cabernet Sauvignon, as a consequence of an unintended field crossing in Bordeaux, most likely in the 18th century.

Almost all dry, unblended Sauvignon Blanc is meant to be drunk young. Sauvignon Blanc pairs well with grilled tuna, salads, and goat cheese.

## here's a way to sweeten tomatoes

if you have tomatoes that aren't sweet enough, add a little salt, a few drops of balsamic vinegar, or even a drop or two of honey to bring out the sweetness.

# tuscan bread salad with tomatoes and basil

Imagine a sandwich of ripe, juicy tomatoes, crisp cucumbers, thin slices of sweet red onion, and sprigs of fresh herbs tucked between two thick slices of crusty European-style bread. Now imagine tearing that sandwich into pieces, dousing it with vinegar and fruity olive oil, and tossing it all together in a bowl. These are the makings of a bread salad called *panzanella,* from Italy.

½ pound coarse-textured bread, 3 to 4 days old

½ cup water

1 cucumber, cut into ½-inch dice

Salt

4 ripe red tomatoes (about 1½ pounds), diced

1 red onion, diced

½ cup (lightly packed) fresh basil leaves

5 tablespoons red wine vinegar

2 cloves garlic, minced

⅓ cup extra virgin olive oil

Freshly ground black pepper

Slice the bread into 1-inch-thick slices. Sprinkle the water over the bread and let sit for 2 minutes. Then carefully squeeze the bread dry. Tear the bread into rough 1-inch pieces and let them rest on paper towels for 20 minutes.

In the meantime, place the cucumbers on a few sheets of paper towels. Sprinkle with salt and let rest for 20 minutes. Then place the cucumbers in a colander and run cold water over them for 1 minute. Dry on clean paper towels.

In a bowl, combine the cucumbers, tomatoes, and onions. Tear the basil into ½-inch pieces and add them to the vegetables. Add the bread and toss carefully.

In a small bowl, whisk together the vinegar, garlic, and olive oil. Season with salt and pepper to taste. Toss with the vegetables and bread; let salad rest 20 minutes.

Arrange the salad on a platter, and serve.                    Serves 6

**Wine Suggestion: Sauvignon Blanc or Pinot Noir**

# a tomato story

When I was six years old, my Mom said to me, "I'm going to make you a tomato sandwich." I asked her, "Oh, why can't you be like other mothers and make me a tuna or peanut butter sandwich?" But she was not deterred.

She went out into the garden (my mother is a fantastic gardener) and picked a few tomatoes, warm from the sun. Back in the kitchen, she toasted some homemade bread and spread it with mayonnaise (probably homemade, knowing her) and then laid thin slices of the tomato on top. She sprinkled the tomato with salt, explaining that "Tomatoes need salt to balance their sweetness and acidity." I thought, "Now, what am I going to do with that information?" Then she put the top on the sandwich, handed it to me, and I took a bite.

I thought I'd died and gone to heaven. And I learned something about balancing flavors.

# fattoush

Salads utilizing leftover bread are made all over the Mediterranean. This one from the Middle East is flavored with sumac (the pleasantly fruity, astringent-flavored berry of the sumac tree) and purslane (a crisp, mild-flavored wild plant). If you cannot find either of these ingredients, simply omit them. The salad will still be delicious.

2 pita breads (8-inch diameter), 3 to 4 days old

1 cucumber, cut into ½-inch dice

Salt

3 ripe tomatoes (about 1¼ pounds), cut into ½-inch dice

6 scallions, white and green parts, thinly sliced

1 green bell pepper, cut into ½-inch dice

1 cup fresh purslane leaves (optional)

¼ cup chopped fresh flat-leaf parsley

⅓ cup chopped fresh mint

¼ cup chopped fresh cilantro

Freshly ground black pepper

2 cloves garlic, minced

¼ cup fresh lemon juice

⅓ cup extra virgin olive oil

2 teaspoons crushed dried sumac (optional)

Preheat the oven to 375°F.

Split each pita bread into 2 rounds, and tear them into 1-inch pieces. Spread them out on a baking sheet, and bake until light golden and dry, 10 to 15 minutes. Set aside.

Place the cucumbers in a single layer on several layers of paper towels. Sprinkle with salt, and let rest for 20 minutes. Then place the cucumbers in a colander, run cold water over them for a moment, and dry them on clean paper towels.

In a bowl, combine the cucumbers with the tomatoes, scallions, bell peppers,

purslane, parsley, mint, and cilantro. Season with salt and pepper, and toss together carefully.

In a small bowl, whisk together the garlic, lemon juice, and olive oil. Season with salt and pepper to taste. Toss the salad, pita crisps, and dressing together. Place on a platter, sprinkle with the sumac, and serve immediately. **Serves 6**

**Wine Suggestion: Pinot Noir or Merlot**

# turkish olive and bread salad

This bread salad came to me from my Turkish friend Angel Stoyanoff. Angel owned a restaurant in San Francisco for several years; both his parents are great cooks; and his brother owns a large bakery on the eastern side of the Bosporus. This salad was a staple of Angel's childhood, something his mother would just throw together and serve alongside lamb shish kebab.

3 ripe tomatoes (about 1¼ pounds), cut into ½-inch dice

1 small red onion, cut into ½-inch dice

1 cup pitted and coarsely chopped brine-cured black olives

¼ cup fresh lemon juice

5 tablespoons extra virgin olive oil

Salt and freshly ground black pepper

½ pound coarse-textured sourdough bread, 2 to 3 days old, sliced ½-inch thick

¼ cup coarsely chopped fresh mint

In a large bowl, combine the tomatoes, onions, olives, lemon juice, olive oil, and salt and pepper to taste. Stir together, and let sit at room temperature for 1 hour.

Tear the bread into ¾- to 1-inch pieces.

Just before serving, add the bread to the tomato mixture and toss well. Sprinkle the mint on top, and serve immediately.

Serves 6

Wine Suggestion: Pinot Noir or Merlot

# chopped salad

I think of this as an old-time salad that requires lots of "jaw work." Because some of the ingredients are raw and all are chopped, it has a lot of crunch—and it has a great combination of flavors. It's the kind of salad that would be good served alongside a grilled steak.

3 tablespoons white wine vinegar

¼ cup extra virgin olive oil

1 small shallot, minced

½ teaspoon grated lemon zest

Salt and freshly ground black pepper

1 small head radicchio, diced

2 small carrots, diced

1 small head escarole, chopped

3 heads Belgian endive, cut into ¼-inch slices

1 cup blue cheese, crumbled (4 ounces)

In a small bowl, whisk together the vinegar, olive oil, shallots, and lemon zest. Season to taste with salt and pepper.

In a large bowl, combine the radicchio, carrots, escarole, and endive. Toss with the dressing. Sprinkle with the blue cheese, and serve immediately.            **Serves 6**

**Wine Suggestion: Cabernet Sauvignon**

# arugula salad with bosc pears, stilton, and verjus

*Verjus* (literally "green juice") refers to a sour liquid made from unripe grapes, alcohol, and sherry vinegar; it is used like vinegar or lemon juice in vinaigrette. With a history that dates to Renaissance or even Medieval times, *verjus* is now making a comeback and can be purchased as "Fusion" in well-stocked markets. I was first introduced to *verjus* by my teacher Madeleine Kamman, back in the 1980s. I make a new batch every year or so, when I can find freshly picked, tart green grapes. *Verjus* has a low acid content, so it's very wine-friendly, and in this salad it marries well with the flavors of the pears and the Stilton and the oakiness of the sherry vinegar.

2 tablespoons *verjus* (see page 147)

1 tablespoon sherry vinegar

3 tablespoons extra virgin olive oil

Salt and freshly ground black pepper

6 cups young arugula leaves

1 small head frisée (4 to 5 ounces), stem ends removed, leaves separated

2 Bosc pears, peeled, halved, cored, and thinly sliced

1½ cups (6 ounces) Stilton cheese, crumbled

In a small bowl, whisk together the *verjus*, sherry vinegar, and olive oil. Season to taste with salt and pepper.

Place the arugula and frisée in a bowl and toss together. Add the pears and the vinaigrette, and toss again. Arrange the salad on a platter, and sprinkle the Stilton over the top. Serve immediately.

Serves 6

Wine Suggestion: Sauvignon Blanc or Pinot Noir

# verjus

20 freshly picked tart green grapes

1 cup homemade green grape juice, as sour as possible (see Note)

½ cup alcohol such as grappa, aquavit, or brandy (90 to 100 proof)

¼ cup sherry vinegar

Prick each grape with a needle. Place them in a half-gallon glass jar.

Pour the grape juice into the jar through a paper coffee filter or a cheesecloth-lined strainer. Add the alcohol and vinegar. Cover the jar with several layers of cheesecloth. Do not disturb it for at least a month.

The *verjus* is ready when the liquid is clear, with a fine layer of sediment at the bottom of the jar. It keeps for several years and ages well.

Makes 1¼ cups

*Note: To make green grape juice, simply place green grapes in a blender and blend until smooth.*

# slow-roasted beet salad with parsley, celery, and fennel

Many people don't like beets, but I think that has to do with the way they are usually cooked. In fact, I'll never forget a woman in one of my cooking classes whose husband loved beets, but who hated them herself until she tried this recipe. (She maintained it saved her marriage.) Roasting accentuates the natural sweetness of beets. Here I put them together with parsley, celery, and fennel for a nice fall or winter salad.

1½ pounds red or gold beets, washed

1 tablespoon water

4 tablespoons extra virgin olive oil

1 cup flat-leaf parsley leaves

3 stalks celery, cut into very thin slices on the sharp diagonal

2 bulbs fennel, cut into paper-thin slices, feathery green tops chopped and reserved

½ small red onion, cut into thin rings

2 tablespoons white wine vinegar or Champagne vinegar

Salt and freshly ground black pepper

Preheat the oven to 350°F.

Place the beets in a shallow baking dish, and drizzle them with the water and 1 tablespoon of the olive oil. Roll the beets to coat them. Cover the pan with foil and roast until the beets are tender when pierced with a knife, 60 to 80 minutes. Let cool.

When the beets are cool enough to handle, peel and cut them into thin slices. Reserve.

In a large bowl, toss together the parsley, celery, sliced fennel, and onion.

In another bowl, whisk together the vinegar and the remaining 3 tablespoons olive oil. Season with salt and pepper to taste. Toss three-fourths of the vinaigrette with the celery mixture, and let sit for 5 minutes. In the meantime, toss the remaining vinaigrette with the beets.

Place the celery mixture on a platter, top with the beets, and garnish with the reserved chopped fennel greens. Serve immediately.

Serves 6

Wine Suggestion: Sauvignon Blanc

# true blue salad

I love any kind of blue cheese in a salad—American Maytag Blue, English Stilton, French Roque-fort, Italian Gorgonzola, Spanish Cabrales. They all have that great pungent blue-green mold that forms when the cheese is aged in caves. For this salad, I've taken all of the elements of a classic cheese plate—Gorgonzola, pears, and pecans—and tossed them with endive, arugula, and a nutty vinaigrette. Served after the main course, this is a perfect palate cleanser before dessert. After all, it's just a cheese course in disguise.

2 pears, preferably Bosc or Bartlett

Unsalted butter

½ cup port wine

1 teaspoon sugar

½ tablespoon hazelnut or walnut oil

1 tablespoon white wine vinegar

3 tablespoons olive oil

Salt and freshly ground black pepper

2 heads Belgian endive

8 cups arugula leaves

½ red onion, thinly sliced

1½ cups (6 ounces) Gorgonzola cheese, crumbled

¼ cup pecan halves, toasted (see page 154)

Preheat the oven to 400°F.

Peel, quarter, and core the pears. Place the pears in a buttered baking pan. Drizzle the port over the pears, and sprinkle with the sugar. Cover the pan with foil, and bake, basting occasionally with the pan juices, until the pears are almost tender when pierced with a knife, 15 to 20 minutes. Remove the pears, reserving the pan juices. Let the pears cool; then cut them into thin slices. Pour the pan juices into a small saucepan, place over high heat, and reduce to 1 tablespoon, 1 to 3 minutes.

In a small bowl, whisk together the reduced pan juices, hazelnut oil, vinegar, and olive oil. Season with salt and pepper to taste.

Cut the tip off one of the endives on the diagonal. Rotating the endive, continue to slice it on the diagonal with the cut side always facing down. Repeat with the second endive.

Toss the pears, endive, arugula, and onions together with the vinaigrette. Place on a platter. Crumble the Gorgonzola over the top, sprinkle with the pecans, and serve.

**Serves 6**

**Wine Suggestion: Sauvignon Blanc**

# romaine salad with oranges, walnuts, and manchego

Manchego is a sheep's-milk cheese from the central mountainous part of Spain. Served very simply in slices, it is one of the most common *tapas* in all of Spain. Here it is shaved into a salad of sweet oranges and walnuts, flavored with a light, nutty dressing. Serve it as a first course.

¾ cup walnut halves

2 tablespoons walnut oil

1 tablespoon sugar

¼ teaspoon salt

2 heads romaine lettuce, outside leaves discarded

4 navel oranges

3-ounce chunk of Manchego or Parmigiano-Reggiano cheese

2 tablespoons sherry vinegar

3 tablespoons extra virgin olive oil

1 shallot, minced

Salt and freshly ground black pepper

Preheat the oven to 375°F.

Place the walnuts in a small bowl. Add 1 tablespoon of the walnut oil and toss to coat. Add the sugar and the ¼ teaspoon salt; toss again. Place the walnuts in a single layer on a baking sheet, and bake until they are lightly browned, 5 to 7 minutes. Reserve.

Separate the leaves of the romaine lettuce. Using mostly the young tender hearts, wash the lettuce and spin dry.

Grate enough zest from one of the oranges to measure 1 teaspoon; reserve the zest. Juice that orange and reserve 3 tablespoons juice. Using a sharp knife, cut the tops and bottoms off the remaining 3 oranges to reveal the flesh. Trim off all of the peel so that no white pith remains. Cut the oranges across into ¼-inch-thick slices. Discard any seeds. Set the slices aside.

Shave the Manchego cheese into a bowl and reserve.

In a small bowl, whisk together the orange zest, orange juice, sherry vinegar, remaining 1 tablespoon walnut oil, the olive oil, and the shallots. Season with salt and pepper to taste.

Toss the romaine leaves with the vinaigrette and arrange on a platter. Scatter the walnuts, Manchego cheese, and orange slices over the top, and serve immediately.

Serves 6

Wine Suggestion: Sauvignon Blanc or Pinot Noir

## toasting nuts

Pecans, walnuts, and almonds:

Preheat the oven to 350°F.

Spread the nuts on a baking sheet and bake until they are fragrant, 5 to 7 minutes.

Pine nuts:

Heat a dry skillet over medium heat. Add the pine nuts and cook, shaking the pan constantly, until the nuts are light golden, 2 to 3 minutes.

# layered salad of bulgur, fennel, pine nuts, dill, and mint

I just love to be invited for dinner, but when you're in my profession, invitations are few and far between. This past summer, a friend invited me to dinner on her terrace overlooking San Francisco Bay. I jumped at the chance and offered to bring something. When the day got closer, I realized that my schedule would be too tight to make something on the day of her dinner party, so I decided to prepare a dish in advance that would still retain the freshness of the season. This is the salad I brought. I carried home an empty bowl—everyone had loved it.

1 cup medium-fine bulgur or cracked wheat

½ cup extra virgin olive oil

4 cloves garlic, minced

1 cup fresh lemon juice

2 teaspoons salt

8 scallions, white and green parts, thinly sliced

1 cup chopped fresh flat-leaf parsley

⅓ cup chopped fresh mint

½ cup chopped fresh dill

2 English (hothouse) cucumbers, peeled, seeded, and cut into ½-inch dice

¼ teaspoon freshly ground black pepper

1 large bulb fennel

⅓ cup pine nuts, toasted (see page 154)

Salt and freshly ground black pepper

Fresh lemon juice

Place the bulgur in a large salad bowl. In a small bowl, whisk together the olive oil, garlic, 1 cup lemon juice, and 1 teaspoon of the salt; drizzle this dressing over the bulgur. Spread the scallions over the bulgur. Continue layering, adding the parsley, mint, dill, and cucumbers. Sprinkle the remaining 1 teaspoon salt and the ¼ teaspoon pepper over the top. Cover with plastic wrap and refrigerate for at least 24 hours and up to 48 hours.

Bring the salad to room temperature.

Meanwhile, cut the fennel bulb in half from top to bottom. Cut the halves into paper-thin crosswise slices. Toss the salad, fennel, and pine nuts together. Season with salt, pepper, and lemon juice to taste, and serve.

Serves 6 to 8

Wine Suggestion: Sauvignon Blanc

# salad of pomegranates, grapes, apples, pears, and pecans with frisée

When autumn arrives, my mind always drifts to this personal favorite, whose colors and flavors exemplify the season. To extract the pomegranate seeds, submerge the quartered pomegranate in cold water and remove the skin and membrane under water. The skin and membrane float to the surface, and the seeds fall to the bottom. Discard the skin and membrane and scoop the seeds from the water! Dry the seeds on paper towels. If you can't find pomegranates, you could use fresh figs or Fuyu persimmons (these are the ones that can be eaten raw).

½ pomegranate

1 tablespoon sherry vinegar

1 tablespoon red wine vinegar

1 tablespoon walnut oil

3 tablespoons extra virgin olive oil

Salt and freshly ground black pepper

4 pears (about 1½ pounds—Bartlett, Red Bartlett, Anjou, Seckel, or Comice), halved, cored, and thinly sliced

2 cups mixed green and red grapes (about ¾ pound), halved

2 green or red apples (about ¾ pound—Cortland, Delicious, Granny Smith, McIntosh, or pippin), halved, cored, and thinly sliced

½ cup pecan halves, toasted (see page 154)

2 bunches frisée (8 to 10 ounces), trimmed and separated

Remove the seeds from the pomegranate (see headnote). Discard the skin and membrane, and reserve the seeds.

In a small bowl, whisk together the sherry vinegar, red wine vinegar, walnut oil, and olive oil. Season with salt and pepper to taste.

Place the pomegranate seeds, pears, grapes, apples, pecans, and frisée in a large bowl. Add the vinaigrette, toss together, and serve immediately.    Serves 6

Wine Suggestion: Beaujolais

# warm frisée salad with pancetta-wrapped endive

Do you like warm salads as much as I do? Make this one from the late fall through the early spring, when endive is in season. The endive is first blanched, then wrapped inside a slice of pancetta and baked. Drizzle with the vinaigrette and serve.

24 paper-thin slices pancetta (6 ounces)

6 large heads Belgian endive (1¼ to 1½ pounds), ends trimmed

3½ tablespoons fresh lemon juice

3 tablespoons extra virgin olive oil

Salt and freshly ground black pepper

2 heads frisée (8 to 10 ounces), stem ends removed, leaves separated

Preheat the oven to 400°F.

Unroll the pancetta. Cut the endive into quarters.

Bring a large pot of salted water to a boil over high heat. Add 2 tablespoons of the lemon juice. Add the endive and cook for 1 minute. Remove the endive with a slotted spoon, and drain well. In a bowl, toss the endive with 1 tablespoon of the olive oil, and season with salt and pepper.

Wrap 1 slice of pancetta around each piece of endive from end to end. Place in a single layer on a baking sheet. Bake on the top shelf of the oven until the endive is tender and the pancetta is crisp, 18 to 20 minutes.

In the meantime, whisk the remaining 1½ tablespoons lemon juice and 2 tablespoons olive oil together in a small bowl. Season with salt and pepper.

Just before serving, toss the vinaigrette with the frisée. Place the frisée on a platter, top with the warm pancetta-wrapped endive, and serve.

Serves 6

Wine Suggestion: Pinot Noir

# sugar snap pea and mint salad
# with prosciutto

Springtime is the best time to buy young, tender sugar snap peas. You can also use blanched fava beans or even asparagus in this salad. Serve it at room temperature on its own, or on the plate with the main course.

1 pound sugar snap peas, ends and strings removed

1 teaspoon Dijon mustard

¼ cup extra virgin olive oil

2 tablespoons red wine vinegar

Salt and freshly ground black pepper

25 large fresh spearmint leaves, very thinly sliced

¼ pound thinly sliced prosciutto, cut into thin strips

Bring a pot of salted water to a boil. Add the sugar snap peas and simmer until tender and crisp, 1 minute. Drain, and cool immediately under cold running water. Drain again.

In a bowl, whisk together the mustard, olive oil, vinegar, and salt and pepper to taste. Add the sugar snap peas and the mint, and toss. Place the salad on a platter, and distribute the prosciutto over the top. Serve immediately.                    **Serves 6**

**Wine Suggestion: Sauvignon Blanc**

# smoked trout and winter citrus salad

Salads don't have to be reserved for summer. What about a winter salad made with smoked trout and an assortment of colorful citrus fruits? The colors are beautiful and the smoked trout adds incredible flavor.

1 lemon

1 lime

1 pink grapefruit

2 blood oranges or seedless oranges

¼ cup extra virgin olive oil

3 tablespoons very thinly sliced fresh chives

Salt and freshly ground black pepper

1 large or 2 small heads frisée, stems removed and leaves separated

8 to 10 ounces smoked trout, skinned, boned, and flaked

## segmenting citrus

Citrus fruits may be segmented for an attractive presentation.

First, cut off the peel, removing all the pith and the outermost membrane of each segment.

Next, hold the peeled fruit over a bowl. Using a small sharp knife, carefully cut between the fruit and the membrane on either side of a segment to free it, letting it drop into the bowl with the juices. When you have released all the segments, discard the membrane.

Grate ¼ teaspoon zest each from the lemon, lime, grapefruit, and one of the oranges. Combine the zests in a medium-size bowl. Squeeze the lemon, and add 2 tablespoons lemon juice to the bowl. Stir in the olive oil and the chives. Season with salt and pepper to taste.

Using a sharp knife, cut the top and bottom off the grapefruit to reveal the flesh. Trim off all of the peel so that no white pith remains. Cut the grapefruit into sections, cutting between the membranes. Discard any seeds. Set aside. Repeat with the blood oranges.

Place the frisée in a large bowl. Add the grapefruit and orange sections. Add the vinaigrette and carefully toss together. Place on a platter and scatter the trout over the top. Serve immediately.

**Serves 6**

**Wine Suggestion: Sauvignon Blanc**

# tuna niçoise

This Niçoise-like salad was inspired by my friend chef Laurence Jossel, and by numerous Friday lunches in outdoor cafés in the south of France. A composed salad that uses the fruits of the sea and the land is nearly ubiquitous on the summer menus of restaurants from Nice to Marseilles. It needs just a little olive oil and red wine vinegar to bring out all the flavors.

2 teaspoons fennel seeds

2 teaspoons coriander seeds

2 teaspoons cumin seeds

¾ teaspoon black peppercorns

½ teaspoon crushed red pepper flakes

2 teaspoons salt

1½ pounds ahi tuna steaks, cut 1-inch thick

1 to 1½ cups extra virgin olive oil

3 slices lemon

1 bay leaf

2 sprigs fresh thyme


Optional garnishes

Aïoli (see page 131)

Black olives

Cooked potatoes

Blanched green beans

Hard-boiled eggs

Roasted red and yellow peppers

Caperberries

Marinated artichoke hearts

Lemon wedges

Place the fennel seeds, coriander seeds, cumin seeds, peppercorns, and red pepper flakes in a dry frying pan over medium heat. Shaking the pan constantly, toast the spices until they are hot to the back of your hand and are aromatic, 60 to 90 seconds. Remove from the heat and allow to cool. Then place the spices in a spice grinder and grind until fine. Add the salt and stir together.

Spread the ground spices on a baking sheet. Press the tuna into the spices, making sure all sides are coated. Place the tuna on a plate, cover with plastic wrap, and let sit in the refrigerator for a minimum of 2 hours or up to 12 hours.

Bring the tuna back to room temperature.

Over medium heat, warm the olive oil, lemon slices, bay leaf, and thyme sprigs in a skillet that's just large enough to hold the tuna. When the lemons begin to sizzle, add the tuna. Reduce the heat to low and simmer the tuna very slowly, turning it once halfway through the cooking, until it is medium-rare, 3 to 4 minutes. Remove the tuna from the oil and let cool. Reserve the oil. Allow the oil to cool, then strain. Flake the tuna into a bowl and pour the reserved oil over it. The tuna can be refrigerated for 3 to 4 days.

Place the tuna on a large serving platter, add some of the garnishes, and serve.

**Serves 6**

**Wine Suggestion: Bandol rosé**

# mains

roasted chicken with candied lemons and golden fennel

grilled chicken with smoked tomato salsa

red wine-braised chicken with tomatoes and olives

chicken rolled with fontina, prosciutto, and sage

grilled chicken salad with sweet and hot peppers, olives, and
capers

magret of duck with fig and shallot compote

spinach ravioli with tomatoes and basil

risotto with oven-roasted tomatoes and basil

penne with tomatoes and herbed ricotta salata

farfalle pasta with lemon chicken and herbs

artichoke and green olive frittata

ten-minute roasted leek and gruyère soufflé

gnocchi soufflé with gorgonzola cream

italian torta rustica

creamy lemon thyme and onion tart

batter-fried crispy fish with garlic sauce

steamed halibut with fragrant herbs

spicy north african mussels

linguine with fresh manila clams, garlic, and calabrian peppers

moroccan grilled shrimp with fusilli

horseradish-crusted salmon with dilled cucumbers with crème
    fraîche

crispy salmon with spiced lentils and herb salad

hazelnut-crusted salmon with fennel salad

moroccan spice–dusted salmon with lemon mint yogurt

grilled lamb with aromatic moroccan salts

lamb shanks, white beans, and tomatoes

braised leg of lamb with artichokes, with lemon and garlic-roasted
    potatoes

rolled veal with italian sausage and winter herbs, with crisp
    polenta triangles

beef braised with zinfandel and winter vegetables

## simple food

**I try not to fuss with food** too much: no sculpted vegetable garnishes or piped purees; no three-dimensional food that falls off the plate when you make your first cut. I like dishes that are approachable, that delight the senses, and that do not place the importance of the chef over that of the food.

Fluting mushrooms has its place, I suppose. But I think food should look like what it is. I like to focus my attention on selecting the foods that are in season and letting their flavors and colors speak for themselves. This is especially important with the main course, which is at the center of the meal.

I wish I could say that I had invented this kind of cooking, but I didn't. It is centuries deep in the traditions of people all over the world; certainly it is true of the cooking in the countries that border the Mediterranean. This is the food that I relate to—like Braised Leg of Lamb with Artichokes, or Risotto with Oven-Roasted Tomatoes and Basil, Crispy Salmon with Spiced Lentils and Herb Salad, or Magret of Duck with Fig and Shallot Compote.

When a dish is highly composed, the experience is all about the chef's artistry—about something external. When it's the food as itself, it draws you into the world of your senses. It's about you and the people with whom you are sharing your meal.

# what makes a wine "food-friendly"?

Imagine that you have ordered a classic delicate sole meunière (fillet of sole in a lemon butter sauce) and the waiter suggests that you have a big, full-bodied, tannic Cabernet Sauvignon with it. You might think the waiter had lost his grip.

But at Beringer Winery, they've served this combination and found that 95 out of 100 people love it—after they've overcome their surprise. What's going on?

According to Jerry Comfort, Beringer's culinary director, "the Cabernet doesn't overpower the sole because the lemon sauce and the seasonings tame the Cabernet, make it milder. So the Cabernet tastes like Cabernet and the sole tastes like sole."

Certain characteristics in food will dramatically change wine. If a dish is too sweet or too sour, it will change the taste of the wine, making it stronger and more tannic (if there are tannins in the wine). Sweeter foods will make a wine taste stronger; saltier and more acidic foods will make a wine taste milder.

Conversely, foods that are very balanced and not too assertive leave the wine tasting as it was intended. And that's the point. If you can balance the sweet and sour extremes in a dish, the wine won't change at all. So you can have any kind of wine you want.

"In general," Comfort says, "dishes that are considered neutral (not too sweet or too sour), or that are sweet but balanced with salt or some acidity, become *more* wine-friendly." Of the two extremes, high-acidity foods tend to be more wine-friendly than sweet ones. Acidity in a dish will overpower the acid in a wine. "If wine changes," Comfort says, "we prefer it to get milder, not stronger."

When you cook, try to balance between the sweet and protein tastes on one end and the salt and sour tastes on the other. The tomatoes in a dish pairing vine-ripened heirloom tomatoes with mozzarella would make any wine more astringent or tannic (if it was a red) or stronger (if it was white). So seasoning the tomatoes with salt will make the dish very wine-friendly because salt bridges the flavors. "If the dish is balanced between those two sides, the wine will taste as it's intended. And most of the time, we enjoy wine because that's the way the winemaker meant it to taste," according to Comfort.

This makes a lot of sense to me. When I cook, I am always balancing the flavors of sweet, sour, bitter, and salty. Food will change the way wine tastes. If you can balance a dish, you will find that many more wines will go with it.

## the basics of wine and food pairing

The pairing of a great wine with a great dish is more than the sum of its parts; it can create a combination of flavors and an experience of living well that is hard to forget. But how do you find the right wine?

Should you try to match flavors, colors, or intensities? A light-bodied wine with a light-bodied dish? A sweet wine with a sweet dish? Do you need to consult an expert? Is there, in fact, such a thing as a perfect match of wine and food?

Jerry Comfort says no. "Wine and food pairing is really subjective and we all look for different things. At Beringer, we've come to the understanding that a person has selected a particular wine because they like

the taste of that wine." And if they don't like the taste of a particular wine, no matter how well matched it is with the dish they're eating, they're not going to like it.

But if there are no rules, what do you do?

The main thing is that "food and wine pairing shouldn't alter the taste of wine, but be a seamless marriage," according to Comfort. Achieving that is easier than you'd think. One way is to match the extremes of a dish with the wine. So if you are having an overtly sweet dish like foie gras with a fruit compote, for instance, you might serve it with a sweet Sauternes; or an extremely sour dish like ceviche with a high-acid wine like Savignon Blanc. But the other way, Comfort says, is to balance the extremities of flavor in a dish so that you can serve the wine you like.

"We have a romantic attachment," Comfort says, "to the idea that certain wines belong with certain foods." But our choices are really much wider. If you pick wines you like and eat foods you like, the rest will fall into place.

# roasted chicken with candied lemons and golden fennel

Lately brining is one of my favorite techniques. It renders the most delicious, succulent, and juicy chicken, reminiscent of the chicken we ate when we were kids. And it isn't difficult—you just need to plan ahead. Once I've brined the chicken, I put the candied lemons under the skin to flavor the meat during roasting. The lemons, which are sautéed in butter until they caramelize, taste both sweet and tart.

¼ cup sugar

½ cup salt

8 cups water

1 roasting chicken (3½ to 4 pounds)

2 tablespoons unsalted butter

2 small lemons, or 1 large lemon, thinly sliced

4 sprigs fresh rosemary

Extra virgin olive oil

Salt and freshly ground black pepper

1 recipe Golden Fennel (recipe follows)

Place the sugar and ½ cup salt in large bowl. Add the water and stir until dissolved. Place the chicken in the bowl. If it isn't completely submerged in the water, add more water until the chicken is covered. Let sit in the refrigerator for 24 hours.

The next day, melt the butter in a large frying pan over medium heat. Add the lemon slices and cook, turning occasionally, until they begin to caramelize and turn light golden, 10 to 15 minutes. Remove from the pan and set aside to cool.

Preheat the oven to 400°F.

Remove the chicken from the brine and pat it dry with paper towels. Using your fingers, carefully separate the skin from the flesh by running your fingers under the skin of the breast and thighs. Be careful not to tear the skin. Insert the lemon slices underneath the skin, placing them over the breast and thighs. Place the rosemary sprigs inside the cavity of the chicken. Truss the chicken with kitchen string. Brush the chicken with olive oil, and season the outside well with salt and pepper. Place the chicken in a roasting pan.

Roast the chicken until it just begins to take on some color, 15 minutes. Reduce the heat to 350°F and continue to cook until the juices run clear when a skewer is inserted into the thickest part of the thigh, about 1 hour.

Remove the chicken from the oven and let it rest for 10 minutes before serving. Serve with the Golden Fennel.

**Serves 4**

**Wine Suggestion: Chardonnay**

## golden fennel

Here fennel is blanched and then grilled until golden, and tossed with lemon zest and parsley.

4 large bulbs fennel, quartered, feathery tops reserved

2 tablespoons extra virgin olive oil

Salt and freshly ground black pepper

¼ teaspoon crushed fennel seeds

2 teaspoons grated lemon zest

1 tablespoon chopped fresh flat-leaf parsley

Bring a saucepan of salted water to a boil. Add the fennel bulbs and simmer until almost tender but still crisp, 3 to 4 minutes. Drain and let cool.

Preheat the broiler, adjusting the shelf so that it is 4 to 5 inches from the heat source.

Chop enough of the fennel greens to make 1 tablespoon. Reserve.

In a bowl, toss together the blanched fennel, the olive oil, and salt and pepper to taste. Place the fennel in a single layer on a baking sheet. Broil the fennel until it is golden and caramelized, 3 to 4 minutes. Turn the fennel and continue to broil until golden and tender, 3 to 5 minutes. Transfer the fennel to a bowl and add the fennel seeds, lemon zest, parsley, reserved chopped fennel greens, and salt and pepper to taste. Toss and serve.

**Serves 6**

# grilled chicken with smoked tomato salsa

One of the best parts of this dish is the tomato salsa, which gets a lot of flavor from roasting the ingredients. I like to put the smoky sauce underneath the chicken, and the salad of parsley and shaved Parmigiano on top; that way, each bite of chicken contains a bit of everything. You could serve roasted potatoes with this.

3 red bell peppers

1 small jalapeño pepper (optional)

5 ripe plum tomatoes

1 large clove garlic, minced

1½ tablespoons red wine vinegar

6 tablespoons extra virgin olive oil

Salt and freshly ground black pepper

6 boneless, skinless chicken breast halves (about 6 ounces each)

1 tablespoon fresh lemon juice

2 cups fresh flat-leaf parsley leaves

2-ounce piece of Parmigiano-Reggiano cheese, thinly shaved

Preheat a charcoal grill.

Place the bell peppers, jalapeño pepper, and tomatoes on a rack 4 inches from the heat source and grill, turning occasionally, until the tomato skins are black and cracked, 3 to 4 minutes. Set the tomatoes aside to cool and continue grilling until the peppers are black, another 4 minutes. (Alternatively, the peppers and tomatoes can be speared on a long-handled fork and grilled over the burner of a gas stove.) Remove the peppers from the grill and place them in a paper or plastic bag; seal, and let steam for 10 minutes.

When they are cool enough to handle, peel the tomatoes and squeeze out excess seeds. Remove the skin, seeds, and membrane from the bell peppers and the jalapeño.

Combine the peppers, tomatoes, garlic, vinegar, and 3 tablespoons of the olive oil in a blender or food processor, and puree. Season with salt and pepper to taste.

Brush the chicken breasts with 2 tablespoons of the olive oil, and place them on the grill rack. Grill until golden on one side, 4 to 5 minutes. Turn the breasts, season with salt and pepper, and continue to grill until golden and cooked through, 4 to 5 minutes.

Meanwhile, whisk the lemon juice and the remaining 1 tablespoon olive oil together in a small bowl. Season with salt and pepper. Add the parsley and Parmigiano, and toss together.

Heat the tomato sauce and spoon onto individual plates. Place the chicken breasts in the center of the sauce, top with the parsley salad, and serve immediately.

**Serves 6**

**Wine suggestion: Sauvignon Blanc or Pinot Noir**

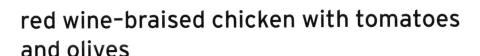

# red wine-braised chicken with tomatoes and olives

This is a great make-ahead dish; it creates its own sauce during cooking and can be easily reheated. It's braised, so the chicken is really tender and juicy. You do want to make sure that you don't overcook the chicken, however. Check it by sticking a skewer, toothpick, or small knife into the thickest part of the breast and thigh. If it goes in and comes out easily, it's done. Serve this with soft polenta (with butter, salt, and pepper to taste), or with mashed potatoes flavored with a few drops of white wine vinegar and extra virgin olive oil instead of the usual butter.

10 cloves garlic, peeled

2 tablespoons olive oil

1 frying chicken (4 pounds), cut into 6 pieces

Salt and freshly ground black pepper

3 cups dry red wine (Cabernet Sauvignon, Chianti, or Côtes du Rhône)

2 cups chicken stock

2 cups peeled, seeded, chopped tomatoes, fresh or canned

1 tablespoon tomato paste

¾ cup Kalamata or Niçoise olives , pitted

3 tablespoons capers, rinsed

Fresh flat-leaf parsley leaves as a garnish

Place the garlic cloves in a saucepan, cover with water, and bring to a boil over medium-high heat. As soon as the water comes to a boil, drain the garlic and discard the water. Repeat. Set the garlic aside.

Heat 1 tablespoon of the olive oil in a large heavy flameproof casserole over medium-high heat. Add the chicken in a single layer, leaving space between the pieces. Season with salt and pepper, and cook until light golden on each side, 10 minutes total. Remove the chicken from the pan and pour off the excess fat. Increase the heat to high, add the wine to the pan, and reduce by approximately half, 10 minutes. Return the drumsticks and thighs to the pan, along with the garlic, chicken stock,

tomatoes, and tomato paste. Bring to a boil, reduce the heat to low, and simmer for 5 minutes. Then add the breasts and continue to cook, covered, until the juices from the chicken are clear, 15 to 20 minutes.

Using tongs, remove the chicken pieces from the pan and set aside; cover with foil to keep warm. Adjust the heat to high, add the olives and capers to the pan, and simmer until the liquid reduces by half and thickens, 10 to 15 minutes. (The chicken and sauce can be prepared ahead to this point and refrigerated. Bring the sauce back to a simmer before continuing.)

Return the chicken to the pan and heat thoroughly, 5 to 10 minutes. Arrange the chicken on a platter and drizzle the sauce over the top. Garnish with parsley, and serve.                                                                                     Serves 6

**Wine Suggestion: Cabernet Sauvignon, Chianti, or Côtes du Rhône**

# chicken rolled with fontina, prosciutto, and sage

This is a wonderful dish to serve guests who appreciate the old favorites. Like a simple black dress with a string of pearls, this dish is stylish and dressy, comforting in its way and always in fashion.

6 boneless, skinless chicken breast halves (about 2 pounds)

Salt and freshly ground black pepper

2 tablespoons chopped fresh sage

6 thin slices prosciutto, cut in half lengthwise

6-ounce chunk of fontina cheese

1 tablespoon extra virgin olive oil

½ cup dry white wine

½ cup chicken stock

Preheat the oven to 400°F.

Using a sharp knife with the blade parallel to the work surface, carefully cut each chicken breast in half, making 2 thin fillets out of one breast. Place the chicken fillets in a single layer, cut side up, on the work surface. Season with salt and pepper. Sprinkle with the sage. Place 1 piece of prosciutto on top of each fillet. With a cheese shaver, shave off 12 slices of fontina. Place 1 piece of fontina in the center of each fillet, on top of the prosciutto. Roll up the fillets, starting at a narrow end and bringing in the edges slightly to form a small parcel. Tie with kitchen string as you would tie ribbon around a present.

Oil a baking dish with the olive oil. Add the chicken rolls and turn to coat them with oil. Bake for 10 minutes. Turn the rolls over, add the wine and chicken stock, and continue to cook until done, another 10 minutes. Remove the chicken from the pan. Pour the pan juices into a skillet and reduce over high heat until they start to thicken, 2 to 3 minutes.

Remove the strings from the chicken rolls, and place 2 rolls on each plate. Spoon the sauce over the top, and serve immediately.

Serves 6

Wine Suggestion: Shiraz

# grilled chicken salad with sweet and hot peppers, olives, and capers

In Italy, this colorful salad goes by the name of *pollo forte*, literally "strong chicken," named for the hot peppers and red pepper flakes that flavor it. It has beautiful color: red, green, and yellow bell peppers, cherry tomatoes, and black olives. Sometimes I'll even add a little cooked penne. It's a great dish for a picnic in the vineyards, or anywhere under a hot sun for that matter.

6 tablespoons extra virgin olive oil

4 skinless, boneless chicken breast halves (6 ounces each)

1 red bell pepper, very thinly sliced

1 green bell pepper, very thinly sliced

1 yellow bell pepper, very thinly sliced

1 pasilla pepper, very thinly sliced (optional)

½ jalapeño pepper, seeded and minced

½ small red onion, thinly sliced

Salt and freshly ground black pepper

2 cloves garlic, minced

½ teaspoon crushed red pepper flakes

3 tablespoons red wine vinegar

2 tablespoons balsamic vinegar

6 ounces assorted cherry tomatoes (red, yellow, orange, pear-shaped, grape shaped), cut in half

½ cup brine-cured black olives, preferably Niçoise or Kalamata

40 fresh basil leaves, cut into thin strips

Heat a charcoal grill.

Brush the chicken breasts with 1 tablespoon of the olive oil. Place the chicken on the grill rack, 4 inches from the heat source, and grill until golden brown, 4 to 5 minutes. Turn the chicken and continue to grill until done, 4 to 5 minutes. Remove and let cool for 20 minutes. Cut the chicken breasts across the grain into very thin strips.

Place them in a bowl and add the bell peppers, pasilla and jalapeño peppers, and onions. Season with salt and pepper, and reserve in the refrigerator.

In a small bowl, whisk together the garlic, red pepper flakes, red wine vinegar, balsamic vinegar, and the remaining 5 tablespoons olive oil. Season with salt and pepper to taste. Add the vinaigrette to the chicken mixture and return to the refrigerator for 15 minutes.

Toss the cherry tomatoes, olives, and basil with the chicken salad. Place in a serving bowl, and serve immediately.

Serves 6 to 8

Wine Suggestion: Pinot Noir or rosé

# magret of duck with fig and shallot compote

I served this to my students (and myself) the first night of our weeklong cooking course at La Combe en Périgord, an 18th-century country house owned and operated by Wendely Harvey and Robert Cave-Rogers in the south of France. It's an impressive and delicious dish, but easy. Serve it with turned (carved in an oval shape) potatoes cooked in duck fat until gold and crispy.

1 tablespoon olive oil

12 shallots, peeled

1 cup fruity red wine (Zinfandel, Merlot, Pinot Noir)

¾ cup chicken stock

12 dried figs (Calimyrna or Smyrna), stems removed

½ teaspoon grated lemon zest

1 tablespoon sugar

Pinch of ground cloves

Salt and freshly ground black pepper

6 duck breast halves with skin (about ½ pound each)

In a skillet over medium heat, warm the olive oil. Add the shallots and cook, stirring occasionally, until golden, 10 minutes. Add the wine, chicken stock, figs, lemon zest, sugar, and cloves. Decrease the heat to low and simmer until the figs are very soft but still retain their shape, about 30 to 45 minutes. Then increase the heat to high and simmer until the sauce thickens, 5 to 10 minutes. Season to taste with salt and pepper. Set aside.

Preheat the oven to 400°F.

Place the duck breasts on a work surface, skin side up. Using a sharp knife, score the skin in a grid pattern, going through half the thickness of the skin but not through to the meat.

Heat a large ovenproof skillet over medium-high heat. Add the duck breasts, skin side down, and cook until the skin is golden and the fat from the skin has rendered, 6 to 8 minutes. Turn the duck breasts over, season with salt and pepper, and transfer the skillet to the oven. Cook until the duck breasts are medium-rare, 6 to 8 minutes.

Remove the skillet from the oven, remove the duck, cover it with foil, and let rest for 10 minutes. In the meantime, warm the fig sauce.

Cut each duck breast on the diagonal into ½-inch-thick slices. Fan the slices out on each plate, spoon the warm sauce over the top, and serve.

Serves 6

Wine Suggestion: Merlot or Syrah

# château mouton-rothschild

I was twenty-four years old and I already knew that I loved food and wine. My best friend and I had just moved into a new apartment, recently vacated by a friend of ours. He'd left us a bottle of Mouton Cadet, a wine of Château Mouton-Rothschild, as a welcoming gift. After we'd unpacked a few boxes, we opened it. As I drank, I noticed something in the bottom of my glass and, with some amazement, realized that it was a fly! I wrote to the winery (little did I know then that it was one of the foremost wineries in the world) and told them about my experience. They wrote back right away, full of apology, and said that if I was ever in France, I must come to the winery and be their special guest for lunch. It happened that my friend and I were planning a trip to France that very summer.

When we arrived in France, we made a beeline to the beautiful Bordeaux wine region, where Château Mouton-Rothschild winery is located. We were taken to an amazing dining room filled with statues of sheep and grand windows that opened out onto rolling vineyards, and there we had the most extraordinary lunch—all the details of which I have never forgotten. We began with croutons topped with duck liver that had been sautéed in butter, and then had breast of duck, and for dessert there was a sumptuous strawberry tart. The wines ranged from a 1966 to a 1918 Château Mouton-Rothschild and, finally, a Château d'Yquem, 1898.

When my friend and I left, we were so overcome by the experience that we sang all the way to Biarritz!

# spinach ravioli with tomatoes and basil

This Tuscan-style dish evokes the European custom of long Sunday lunches gathered around the family table. In fact, pasta made with eggs is almost always reserved for special occasions in Italy. You'll want to perpare this dish in the summertime, when the tomatoes are sweetest and will best complement the delicious ravioli filling of spinach, ricotta, mascarpone, and a little fresh mint. Don't forget to go for your *passeggiata,* or leisurely walk, as Italians would say, after the meal!

Filling

2 pounds fresh spinach, washed, stems trimmed, patted dry

1 tablespoon water

½ pound ricotta cheese

½ pound mascarpone cheese

¾ cup grated Parmigiano-Reggiano cheese

1 egg

3 egg yolks

1 clove garlic, minced

1 tablespoon chopped fresh mint

Salt and freshly ground black pepper

Pinch of freshly grated nutmeg

Tomato sauce

3 tablespoons extra virgin olive oil

5 cloves garlic, crushed with the side of a knife

2½ pounds peeled, seeded, chopped fresh or canned tomatoes (about 4 cups)

Salt and freshly ground black pepper

1 recipe Spinach Pasta Dough (recipe follows)

3 tablespoons unsalted butter

1 cup grated Parmigiano-Reggiano cheese

20 large fresh basil leaves, cut into thin strips

Place the spinach in a large frying pan and sprinkle the water over it. Cover, place over medium-high heat, and wilt the spinach, tossing occasionally, 2 to 3 minutes. Drain the spinach, and remove as much remaining moisture as possible by pressing the spinach between sheets of paper towels until almost dry. Chop the spinach and place it in a large bowl. Add the ricotta, mascarpone, Parmigiano, whole egg, egg yolks, garlic, and mint. Stir together until well mixed. Season with salt, pepper, and nutmeg. Place in the refrigerator until needed.

For the sauce, warm the olive oil in a saucepan over medium-high heat. Add the garlic and cook, stirring frequently, until light golden, about 3 minutes. Remove the garlic with a slotted spoon and discard. Reduce the heat to medium-low, add the tomatoes, and cook just until the tomatoes are heated through, 3 to 4 minutes. Season with salt and pepper. Set aside.

Divide the pasta dough into 4 pieces. Using a pasta machine, roll one piece of the pasta out to $\frac{1}{16}$-inch thickness, or so you can almost see your hand through it. Place the piece of pasta on a floured work surface.

Place 1 heaping tablespoon of the filling just below the center of the sheet. Place another heaping tablespoon 1½ inches away. Continue all the way down the sheet. The sheet should hold approximately 10 mounds of filling. Spray a very light mist of water around the edges, or use a pastry brush to brush the edges lightly with water. Fold the top over the filling so the edges meet. With your fingers, press around each mound of filling to seal the ravioli. Using a zigzag cutter, cut out square ravioli. Place a kitchen towel on a baking sheet, flour it heavily, and place the ravioli on it. Repeat with the remaining dough and filling.

Melt the butter in a small saucepan.

Bring a large pot of salted water to a boil. Add the ravioli and cook until al dente, 3 to 4 minutes. Drain, and toss with the butter. Place the ravioli on a platter, and spoon the warm tomato sauce over the top. Sprinkle with the Parmigiano and basil, and serve immediately.

Makes about 30 ravioli; serves 5

Wine Suggestion: Shiraz or Chianti

# spinach pasta dough

½ pound spinach, washed, stems trimmed, patted dry

1 egg

1 egg yolk

2½ cups all-purpose flour

½ teaspoon salt

Place the spinach, whole egg, and egg yolk in a blender and process until completely smooth. It should measure approximately 1 cup.

Place the flour and ¼ teaspoon of the salt in a mound on a work surface, and make a well in the center. Place the spinach mixture in the well. Using a fork or your thumb and first finger, gradually bring the flour in from the sides, blending it into the spinach until the mixture thickens. The dough should hold together in a ball; if it doesn't, add 1 to 2 tablespoons water. Then use a pastry scraper to incorporate the remaining flour. The dough should be fairly dry but still hold together. (Alternatively, the dough can be made in a food processor. Add 1 to 2 tablespoons less of the spinach mixture, and process until the dough looks crumbly in texture.)

Turn the dough out onto a well-floured work surface and knead it until it is smooth, 4 to 5 minutes. If it sticks to your fingers or to the work surface, knead in additional flour.

Wrap the dough in plastic wrap and let it rest at room temperature for 30 minutes, in the refrigerator for 1 day, or in the freezer for 1 month.

**Makes 1 pound pasta dough**

# risotto with oven-roasted tomatoes and basil

Some people don't like risotto. For others it's a comfort food they could eat every day. I'm some-where in between and find that it all depends on what is added to it. I love it cooked with shrimp, zucchini and squash blossoms, or Amarone wine, as it's made in Italy. Or, as in this recipe, with oven-roasted tomatoes and fresh basil.

2 ripe red tomatoes, cored

3 cups chicken stock

3 cups water

2 tablespoons extra virgin olive oil

1 yellow onion, minced

1½ cups arborio, vialone nano, or carnaroli rice

¾ cup dry white wine

Salt and freshly ground black pepper

1 tablespoon balsamic vinegar

3 tablespoons chopped fresh flat-leaf parsley

1 cup oven-roasted tomatoes (see page 134), cut into quarters

2 tablespoons unsalted butter

20 fresh basil leaves, cut into thin strips

Fresh basil sprigs as a garnish

Using a coarse grater, grate the ripe tomatoes into a saucepan. Discard the skins. Add the chicken stock and water, and bring to a boil over high heat on the back burner of the stove. Reduce the heat to low, and maintain the mixture at just below the boiling point.

Heat the olive oil in a large heavy flameproof casserole over medium heat. Add the onions and cook until soft, 7 minutes. Add the rice and stir constantly for 3 minutes.

Add the wine and simmer until almost evaporated, 3 to 5 minutes. Add about 1 cup of the hot broth and cook, stirring the rice constantly to wipe it away from the bottom and sides of the pot. When more than half of the broth has been absorbed but the rice is still loose, add another ladle of broth and continue to cook the risotto. Season with salt and pepper to taste. Continue to add broth a ladle at a time, stirring constantly, until the rice is chalky in the center, 15 to 18 minutes. If you run out of stock, use hot water.

Add the balsamic vinegar and parsley, and continue to add broth until the center of the rice is tender and no longer chalky, 3 to 5 minutes. Add the oven-roasted tomatoes, another ladle of broth, the butter, and the basil. Stir together. Remove from the heat, cover, and let sit for 5 minutes.

Spoon the risotto onto a large serving platter, garnish with basil sprigs, and serve immediately.                                                     **Serves 6**

**Wine Suggestion: Pinot Noir, Merlot, or Chianti**

# penne with tomatoes and herbed ricotta salata

This is a great dish to prepare when someone comes by unexpectedly for a weeknight dinner; it's very quick and has lots of flavor. The ricotta salata is simply salted, drained, and dried ricotta cheese. It's not an overpowering cheese, but it has a lot of saltiness and gives body to a dish. It pairs really well with tomatoes and herbs.

1½ cups (¾ pound) ricotta salata, crumbled

2 tablespoons chopped fresh basil

2 tablespoons chopped fresh chives

1 tablespoon chopped fresh mint

1 teaspoon chopped fresh oregano

1 teaspoon chopped fresh thyme

¼ cup extra virgin olive oil

3 tablespoons balsamic vinegar

Salt and freshly ground black pepper

1½ pounds assorted cherry tomatoes (red, orange, yellow, green, plum), cut in half

¾ pound dried penne pasta

Crumble the ricotta salata into a bowl. Add the basil, chives, mint, oregano, and thyme. Mix together until the cheese is coated with the herbs. Reserve.

In a large bowl, whisk together the olive oil and vinegar. Season to taste with salt and pepper. Add the tomatoes, toss thoroughly, and let sit for 10 minutes.

Meanwhile, bring a large pot of salted water to a boil. Add the penne and cook until al dente, about 10 minutes or according to directions on package. Drain, and place the pasta in a bowl. Immediately add the tomatoes and vinaigrette and the cheese mixture, and toss together. Serve immediately.

Serves 6

Wine Suggestion: Sauvignon Blanc

# farfalle pasta with lemon chicken and herbs

My assistant, Bruce Fielding, says this is his favorite of all my recipes. It's a bit unusual: You combine herbs, arugula, parsley, cilantro, basil, and mint with the hot pasta and grilled chicken. The herbs wilt and create a pasta dish that is *so* satisfying.

⅓ cup plus 1 tablespoon extra virgin olive oil

3 tablespoons fresh lemon juice

3 cloves garlic, minced

¾ teaspoon ground cumin

Salt and freshly ground black pepper

3 skinless, boneless chicken breast halves (about ¾ pound)

3 cups chicken stock

¾ pound farfalle (bow-tie) pasta

½ cup fresh flat-leaf parsley leaves

¾ cup fresh cilantro leaves

¾ cup fresh basil leaves, torn into large pieces

½ cup fresh mint leaves

1½ cups fresh arugula leaves

1 preserved lemon, cut into ¼-inch dice (optional; recipe follows)

If you are cooking indoors, heat a ridged cast-iron grill over medium heat for 10 minutes. Otherwise, start a charcoal grill.

In a large bowl, whisk the ⅓ cup olive oil with the lemon juice, garlic, cumin, and salt and pepper to taste. Reserve.

Using the remaining 1 tablespoon olive oil, oil the chicken breasts. Cook the chicken on the grill until golden on one side, 3 to 4 minutes. Turn the chicken over, season with salt and pepper, and cook until done, 4 to 5 minutes. Cut the chicken across the grain into thin slices. Reserve.

Place the chicken stock in a saucepan and boil over medium-high heat 10 to 15 minutes until reduced to 1 cup. Add the reserved oil/lemon juice mixture and set aside.

Bring a large pot of salted water to a boil. Add the farfalle and cook until al dente, 10 to 12 minutes. Drain the pasta and toss it immediately with the stock mixture. Add the chicken slices, parsley, cilantro, basil, mint, arugula, preserved lemon, and salt and pepper to taste. Toss well, place on a platter, and serve immediately.

Serves 6 to 8

Wine Suggestion: Sauvignon Blanc

## preserved lemons

Preserved lemons are essential to the Moroccan kitchen, where they are used in tagines (stews) and salads. I use them in many other dishes as well, to add a special flavor. It is predominantly the skin of the preserved lemon, not the pulp, that is used.

Preserved lemons are best made with Meyer lemons—the smooth, shiny, mildly acidic, orange-yellow-skinned lemons that are available during the winter months in California and Florida and at specialty greengrocers around the country. Eureka and Lisbon lemons, the kind commonly found in grocery stores, can also be preserved, but they take longer because of their thicker skins. If you can't find Meyer lemons, or can't wait a month to preserve them, you can find good-quality preserved lemons at specialty food markets.

    8 Meyer lemons, washed
    ½ cup kosher salt
    2 cinnamon sticks, each 2 to 3 inches
    4 bay leaves
    Fresh lemon juice (Eureka, Lisbon, or Meyer)

Cut each lemon into quarters from the top to within ½ inch of the bottom, taking care to leave the four sections joined at the stem end. Sprinkle the insides of the lemon with some of the kosher salt.

Place 1 tablespoon of the salt in a 1-quart canning jar and pack the lemons into the jar, adding the remaining salt, the cinnamon sticks, and the bay leaves as you go. Push down on the lemons to release as much juice as possible. Add extra juice as needed to almost reach the top of the jar. Cover the jar tightly. Let the lemons sit at room temperature for 1 month, turning the jar upside-down periodically to distribute the salt and juices.

Some white crystals will form on top of the lemons in the jar; this is normal—do not discard the lemons. They can be stored at room temperature or refrigerated, and will keep for up to 1 year. To use a lemon, remove it from the brine and discard the pulp. Wash the peel, and use as directed. **Makes 1 quart jar**

# artichoke and green olive frittata

Imagine that you're in Italy; it's Sunday night–many hours after the big noon meal–and you want a little bite of something. A frittata is just the right thing, and every Italian home would have on hand everything needed to make one. In France they would call it an omelette; in Spain, a tortilla. And in all three countries, this dish might be served as a first course as well.

3 tablespoons extra virgin olive oil

2 cloves garlic, minced

8 eggs

10 small artichoke hearts cured in olive oil, sliced

⅓ cup coarsely chopped pitted cured green olives

1 teaspoon grated lemon zest

1 teaspoon chopped fresh thyme

1 teaspoon chopped fresh sage

½ cup grated Parmigiano-Reggiano cheese

Salt and freshly ground black pepper

In a small skillet, warm 1 tablespoon of the olive oil. Add the garlic and cook until it just starts to soften, 30 seconds. Immediately remove from the heat and pour the oil and garlic into a large bowl. Add the eggs to the bowl and whisk together.

Add the artichokes, olives, lemon zest, thyme, sage, and Parmigiano. Season with salt and pepper to taste.

Preheat the oven to 400°F.

Heat the remaining 2 tablespoons olive oil in a 10-inch nonstick ovenproof omelette pan over medium heat until it is hot but not smoking. Add the frittata mixture, and using a spatula, press on it to make an even cake. Cook until the bottom is golden and set but the top is still runny, 8 to 10 minutes. During the cooking, occasionally lift the outer edges so the runny egg can run underneath. Transfer the pan to

the oven and cook until the eggs are set and golden brown, 6 to 7 minutes. Let set for 5 minutes in the pan.

Invert the frittata onto a serving platter. Cut it into wedges and serve hot, warm, or at room temperature.

Serves 4

Wine Suggestion: Sauvignon Blanc

# the fifth flavor: what is it?

When I compose a dish, I am always looking to balance flavors—a sweet tomato with a sprinkle of salt and a splash of balsamic vinegar; pizza with sweet caramelized onions, bitter walnuts, and salty gorgonzola. Dishes that are balanced taste better and are more wine-friendly.

The flavors of sweet, sour, bitter, and salty are considered to be the four primary tastes (that is, tastes that aren't produced from a combination of others). But lately both neuroscientists and many chefs are acknowledging that there may be a *fifth* flavor: *umami* (pronounced ooh-mammy).

*Umami*, like many things, is difficult to define, but you know it when you taste it. It's the savory flavor that gives dry-aged steak, lobster, shiitake mushrooms, soy sauce, Parmigiano-Reggiano, or Gruyere that certain something. Dishes that are balanced with an *umami* component seem to have an extra dimension of flavor.

To balance flavors in your cooking, think about sweet, sour, bitter, salty, and *umami* tastes.

# ten-minute roasted leek and gruyère soufflé

Get your guests to the table and then serve them this ingenious soufflé that bakes in ten minutes rather than the customary sixty! We used to make a soufflé like this at Chez Panisse and it really is amazing, especially when it's baked in a beautiful oval ovenproof platter, such as one of the French porcelain platters that are widely available in this country. It makes a great main course with a salad—or it can be a first course.

> 2 tablespoons extra virgin olive oil
>
> 4 leeks, white and 2 inches green part, cut into ¼-inch dice
>
> 1 teaspoon chopped fresh thyme
>
> Salt and freshly ground black pepper
>
> 2½ cups half-and-half
>
> 5 tablespoons unsalted butter
>
> 5 tablespoon all-purpose flour
>
> 6 eggs, separated, room temperature
>
> 1 cup (4 ounces) grated Gruyère cheese
>
> 1 cup finely grated Parmigiano-Reggiano cheese

Warm the olive oil in a large skillet over medium-high heat. Add the leeks, thyme, and salt and pepper to taste. Reduce the heat to low and cook, stirring occasionally, until the leeks are soft and just starting to turn lightly golden, 40 to 45 minutes. Remove from the heat and let cool.

Pour the half-and-half into a saucepan and bring it almost to the boiling point.

Meanwhile, melt the butter in a heavy saucepan over medium heat. Add the flour and whisk 1 to 2 minutes. Add the scalded half-and-half to the flour mixture, stirring rapidly with a whisk. Cook for 3 to 4 minutes, until the sauce is smooth and thick. Add salt and pepper to taste.

Add the egg yolks to the cream sauce, one at a time, stirring well after each addition. Add the Gruyère, ½ cup of the Parmigiano, and salt and pepper to taste. Add the cooled leeks to the cream sauce. Mix well.

Preheat the oven to 450°F.

While the oven is heating, place the egg whites in a clean bowl and beat until they form stiff peaks. Fold half of the whites into the cheese mixture with as few strokes as possible. Then fold in the remaining whites. Pour the mixture onto a generously buttered 18-inch oval ovenproof dish (or two 12-inch ovals). Sprinkle the top with the remaining ½ cup Parmigiano. Bake on the top shelf of the oven until puffed and well browned, 10 to 14 minutes.

Serves 8

Wine Suggestion: Pinot Noir or Cabernet Sauvignon

# gnocchi soufflé with gorgonzola cream

Gnocchi (pronounced *n'yohk*-kee; the word means "dumplings") can be made of many things—potatoes, butternut squash, or semolina, to name a few. But this version is made with cream puff dough that you pipe into boiling water, drain, and then bake with Gorgonzola cream. They are cooked until they are golden and puffed up, and they absolutely melt in your mouth.

> 2 cups milk
> 14 tablespoons (1¾ sticks) unsalted butter
> ½ teaspoon salt
> 1½ cups all-purpose flour
> 6 eggs
> 1½ cups heavy cream
> 1¼ cups (5 ounces) Gorgonzola cheese, crumbled
> Salt and freshly ground black pepper
> ¼ cup grated Parmigiano-Reggiano cheese

Bring the milk, butter, and ½ teaspoon salt to a boil in a large heavy saucepan over medium-high heat. Reduce the heat to medium-low, add the flour all at once, and mix vigorously with a wooden spoon until the dough separates from the edges of the pan and forms a ball, 2 to 3 minutes. Remove the pan from the heat. While the dough is still warm, add the eggs, one at a time, beating well with a wooden spoon after each addition until the dough no longer looks shiny.

Fill a large shallow saucepan with salted water and bring to a boil. Reduce the heat and maintain at a simmer.

Fit a large pastry bag with a ¾-inch plain round tip and fill it with the dough. Holding a paring knife at the tip, cut off 1-inch pieces of dough and let them drop into the simmering water. Simmer gently until they begin to puff and are cooked through, about 5 minutes. Remove the gnocchi with a slotted spoon, and plunge them directly into ice water to chill thoroughly. Drain well. (The gnocchi will keep well at this

stage, covered, in the refrigerator for up to 2 days. Toss them with 1 tablespoon olive oil before refrigerating.)

Preheat the oven to 450°F.

In a shallow heavy saucepan, bring the cream, Gorgonzola, and salt and pepper to taste to a boil. Simmer until the cream thickens slightly, 6 to 8 minutes. Add the gnocchi and the Parmigiano, and heat gently. Taste, and season with salt and pepper. Pour the gnocchi and cream into a buttered 10-inch oval baking dish and bake until they puff and are golden, 10 minutes. Serve immediately.                **Serves 8**

**Wine Suggestion: Cabernet Sauvignon**

# italian torta rustica

This torta takes a little bit of work, but it makes enough for ten hungry Italians (should you ever find yourself in need of feeding such a group). The dough is simple to make and encases a deep pie filled with cheeses, sliced meats, and vegetables. At its center is ricotta cheese mixed with wilted greens. It's great picnic food: Make it ahead and serve it with the Grilled Chicken Salad with Sweet and Hot Peppers, Olives, and Capers (page 180).

**Dough**
1¼ teaspoons dry yeast
3¼ cups all-purpose flour
1 teaspoon salt
1¼ cups warm water (115°F)
¼ cup extra virgin olive oil

**Filling**
1½ pounds mixed greens (Swiss chard, spinach, mustard greens, escarole, beet greens), stems removed, rinsed but not dried
4 tablespoons extra virgin olive oil
1 pound button mushrooms, thinly sliced
4 cloves garlic, minced
Salt and freshly ground black pepper
2 red bell peppers, thinly sliced
2 yellow onions, thinly sliced
1 pound ricotta cheese, drained overnight in a cheesecloth-lined strainer
1 egg, lightly beaten
3 cups (¾ pound) mozzarella cheese, grated
2 cups (½ pound) fontina cheese, grated
¾ pound assorted cured meats (prosciutto, salami, capocollo, mortadella), thinly sliced
1 teaspoon olive oil

Prepare the dough: Place the yeast, flour, and salt in a food processor. With the motor running, slowly add the warm water. Then quickly add the olive oil and process until the dough is smooth and evenly soft, about 45 seconds. If the dough is dry and rough and doesn't form a ball, add a tablespoon or two of water. (The dough can also be made in an electric mixer using the same technique. Instead of processing the dough for 45 seconds, knead the dough on low speed using the dough hook.)

Place the dough in an oiled bowl and turn to coat it with oil. Cover tightly with plastic wrap and set aside in warm place (70° to 75°F) until doubled in volume, 1 hour.

In the meantime, prepare the filling: Heat a large skillet, add the greens, and toss with tongs until wilted, 3 to 6 minutes. Squeeze the greens in a kitchen towel to remove the excess moisture. Chop the greens coarsely and set aside.

Heat 2 tablespoons of the olive oil in a frying pan over medium-high heat. Add the mushrooms and garlic and sauté until the liquid from the mushrooms has completely evaporated, 15 minutes. Season with salt and pepper to taste, remove from the pan, and set aside in a large bowl.

Add the remaining 2 tablespoons olive oil to the pan and cook the peppers and onions over medium heat until soft, 15 minutes. Add to the mushrooms and toss together.

In a bowl, stir together the ricotta, beaten egg, and reserved greens. Season with salt and pepper to taste, and set aside. Combine the mozzarella and fontina in another bowl and set aside.

Preheat the oven to 400°F.

Assemble the *torta:* Place a 10-inch springform pan on a baking sheet and brush the inside with the 1 teaspoon olive oil. Punch down the dough and divide it into 2 pieces, one of which is three quarters of the volume and the other is one quarter. On a floured surface, roll the larger piece out to form a 16-inch circle. Transfer it to the springform pan, pressing the dough against the bottom and sides and allowing it to hang over the edges.

Arrange one fourth of the meat slices on the bottom of the pan and top with one fourth of the grated cheese. Next, layer half of the mushroom/pepper mixture on top of the cheese. Sprinkle with one fourth of the grated cheese. Place another layer of the meats on top of that. Spread the ricotta/greens mixture over the meat. Repeat the sequence of layers, ending with the meat.

Roll the remaining dough out to form a 10-inch circle. Brush the overhanging dough lightly with water. Cover with the top crust. Pinch the crusts together and crimp to form a decorative edge. With a sharp knife, cut two ½-inch vents in the middle of the top crust. Bake on the lowest rack of the oven for 1¼ hours. Let cool for 30 to 45 minutes before slicing. Serve hot or at room temperature. Serves 10

**Wine Suggestion: Chardonnay or Merlot**

*Note: If the top crust is getting too dark while it is baking, place a piece of foil loosely over the top.*

# creamy lemon thyme and onion tart

Lemon thyme has a wonderful flavor, but you can also use regular thyme in this dish. You could serve this as a main course, either hot out of the oven or at room temperature, with a simple salad, or as a first course.

1 tablespoon unsalted butter

1 large yellow onion, thinly sliced

1 tablespoon chopped fresh lemon thyme or thyme

Salt and freshly ground black pepper

½ cup heavy cream

1 cup sour cream

¾ cup (3 ounces) Gruyère cheese, grated

2 eggs, lightly beaten

¼ cup thinly sliced fresh chives

One prebaked 9-inch Short Crust Tart Shell (recipe follows)

Melt the butter in a frying pan over medium heat. Add the onions and lemon thyme and cook, stirring occasionally, until very soft and light golden, 25 minutes. Season with salt and pepper to taste. Let cool.

Preheat the oven to 400°F.

In a bowl, stir together the heavy cream, sour cream, Gruyère, eggs, and chives. Add the onions and stir together. Season with salt and pepper. Pour the mixture into the prepared tart shell.

Place the tart in the oven and bake for 10 minutes. Then turn the heat down to 375°F and continue to bake for another 15 to 20 minutes, or until the top is golden and firm to the touch. Let the tart rest for 20 minutes before serving.          Serves 4

**Wine Suggestion: Chardonnay**

# short crust tart shell

8 tablespoons (1 stick) unsalted ice-cold butter, cut into 1-inch pieces

1⅛ cups all-purpose flour

⅛ teaspoon salt

¼ cup ice water

Using the paddle attachment on an electric mixer (or in the bowl of a food processor), blend the butter and flour at low speed (or pulse several times) until the mixture resembles coarse meal. Mix the salt and ice water together, and add to the flour mixture. Blend (or pulse) just until the dough comes together, stopping once, soon after you start mixing, to scrape the bowl. Wrap the dough in plastic wrap and let it rest in the refrigerator for at least 30 minutes or as long as overnight.

On a floured surface, roll the pastry out to form an 11-inch circle. Fit the dough into the tart pan and crimp the edges. Place it in the freezer for 30 minutes, or wrap it in plastic wrap and freeze it for up to 2 weeks.

Preheat the oven to 400°F.

Line the pastry with baking parchment, and scatter 1 cup dry beans or pie weights over the parchment. Bake the tart shell until the top edges are light golden, 10 to 15 minutes. Remove the parchment and weights, reduce the heat to 375°F, and continue to bake until the shell is light golden, 15 to 20 minutes.          **Makes one 9-inch tart shell**

# batter-fried crispy fish with garlic sauce

The combination of hot crispy fish with this garlicky sauce is really marvelous. The sauce, called *skorthalia,* in Greece, is similar to one served with pita crisps in the Firsts chapter; this is a more traditional version. *Skorthalia* is linked to France's *aïoli* and *rouille* and to Spain's *allioli* and *romesco*—they all feature an abundance of mashed garlic. But unlike those other garlic sauces, *skorthalia* has a starchy base of either mashed potatoes or nuts and soaked bread, as in this recipe.

2 thick slices coarse-textured white bread, crusts removed

2 cups water

½ cup walnut halves or pieces

Salt

2 tablespoons vegetable oil

2 tablespoons extra virgin olive oil

2 tablespoons white wine vinegar

2 tablespoons mayonnaise

2 large cloves garlic

Freshly ground black pepper

2¼ cups all-purpose flour

1 teaspoon baking powder

1¼ cups flat warm beer

Olive oil for frying

2 pounds boneless rock cod or halibut

Lemon wedges

Place the bread in a bowl, pour the water over it, and then immediately remove the bread. Squeeze the bread to remove the excess moisture. Discard the water.

Grind the walnuts in a food processor or blender; you should have ¼ cup. Add the bread, salt to taste, vegetable and olive oils, 1 tablespoon of the vinegar, the mayonnaise, and the garlic. Puree to form a smooth paste. If the mixture is too thick, thin it

with 1 to 2 tablespoons water. Taste, and season with salt, pepper, and additional vinegar if desired. Place the sauce in a serving bowl and reserve in the refrigerator.

In a large bowl, whisk together 1¼ cups of the flour, salt and pepper to taste, the baking powder, and the beer. The batter should be the consistency of pourable pancake batter; add more water if necessary.

Heat 3 inches of olive oil in a deep pot until it is 375° to 400°F, or until a drop of the batter sizzles and turns golden brown on contact.

Cut the fish into 2-inch pieces. Place the remaining 1 cup flour in a bowl and dredge the fish in the flour. Pat off the excess. Dip the fish pieces into the batter, and fry in the hot oil 1 to 2 minutes, until golden brown and crispy. Remove the fish from the oil and drain on paper towels.

Serve the fish immediately, with the garlic sauce and lemon wedges alongside.

Serves 6

Wine Suggestion: Sauvignon Blanc

# steamed halibut with fragrant herbs

Poaching is back! It's such a great technique for cooking fish, especially when we're all interested in lighter foods that don't use fat in the cooking but still have lots of flavor. In this dish, I place the halibut fillets between layers of parsley and fennel, and then steam them over herb-infused wine. I like to serve the fish with a sauce full of Sicilian flavors—raisins, pine nuts, fennel, and lemon zest. In Italy they call this combination of sweet and sour flavors *agrodolce*.

> 3 cups dry white wine
>
> ¼ cup golden raisins
>
> ¼ cup pine nuts
>
> 4 shallots, minced
>
> ½ cup diced fresh fennel (¼-inch dice)
>
> 2 teaspoons grated lemon zest
>
> 1 tablespoon fresh lemon juice
>
> 5 tablespoons extra virgin olive oil
>
> Salt and freshly ground black pepper
>
> 1½ to 2 pounds halibut fillets, cut into 6 pieces
>
> 1 cup (loosely packed) fresh flat-leaf parsley leaves
>
> 1½ cups thinly sliced fennel
>
> 2 cups water
>
> 8 sprigs fresh thyme
>
> 3 bay leaves
>
> Lemon wedges as a garnish
>
> Fresh flat-leaf parsley sprigs as a garnish

In a small saucepan over medium-high heat, simmer 1 cup of the wine and the raisins until only 2 tablespoons of the wine remain and the raisins are soft, 3 to 5 minutes. Reserve.

In a small dry skillet, toast the pine nuts over medium heat, stirring constantly, until golden, 2 to 3 minutes.

In a small bowl, stir together the white wine mixture, pine nuts, half of the shallots, the diced fennel, lemon zest, lemon juice, and 3 tablespoons of the olive oil. Season with salt and pepper to taste. Reserve to serve with the fish.

Using 1 tablespoon of the olive oil, lightly oil the halibut pieces. Rub them with salt and pepper. Using the remaining 1 tablespoon olive oil, lightly oil the tray that sits inside the fish poacher. (If you don't have a fish poacher, use a large sauté pan with a fitted lid, lightly oiling the bottom of the pan.) Spread half of the parsley leaves and half of the sliced fennel on the tray. Arrange the fish in a single layer on top of the herbs. Top with the remaining parsley and fennel. Pour the remaining 2 cups wine and the water into the bottom of the fish poacher. Add the remaining shallots, the thyme sprigs, and the bay leaves to the liquid. Place the tray in the poacher. The liquid should come just to the level of the tray but should not cover the fish.

Place the fish poacher over two burners and bring the liquid to a boil over high heat. Reduce the heat to low, cover, and simmer until the fish is cooked through, 6 to 9 minutes, depending upon the thickness of the fillets. Remove the poacher from the heat. Remove the tray, and discard the liquid, parsley, and sliced fennel.

Place a piece of fish on each plate, and top with the sauce. Garnish with lemon wedges and parsley sprigs, and serve immediately.                    Serves 6

**Wine Suggestion: Chardonnay**

# spicy north african mussels

Mussels are assertive enough for the fragrant and colorful spices of North Africa. Be sure to have plenty of crusty bread on hand to soak up the delectable juices.

3 tablespoons extra virgin olive oil

1 small red onion, finely minced

5 cloves garlic, minced

2 teaspoons ground cumin

1½ teaspoons ground ginger

¾ teaspoon turmeric

¾ teaspoon sweet paprika

1 teaspoon harissa (see headnote, page 230)

Salt and freshly ground black pepper

1½ cups peeled, seeded, chopped tomatoes, fresh or canned

1½ cups fish stock or bottled clam juice

3 pounds mussels, scrubbed, beards removed

¼ cup chopped fresh cilantro

1 to 2 tablespoons fresh lemon juice

Fresh cilantro sprigs as a garnish

Heat the olive oil in a large skillet over medium heat. Add the onions and sauté until soft, 10 minutes. Add the garlic, cumin, ginger, turmeric, paprika, harissa, and salt and pepper to taste. Cook, stirring constantly, for 2 minutes. Add the tomatoes and fish stock. Simmer slowly, uncovered, for 15 minutes. Remove from the heat and allow to cool slightly.

Puree the tomato mixture in a blender until smooth. Return the puree to the skillet and place it over medium-high heat. Add the mussels, cover, and simmer until the shells open, 3 to 5 minutes. As the mussels open, remove them with tongs. When all of the mussels have opened, boil the cooking liquid over high heat until it has reduced by one-quarter. Add the cilantro and lemon juice.

Place the mussels in a bowl and pour the sauce over them. Garnish with cilantro sprigs, and serve immediately.                    Serves 6

**Wine Suggestion: Merlot, Zinfandel, or Cotês du Rhône**

# linguine with fresh manila clams, garlic, and calabrian peppers

Some of the simplest dishes can be the toughest to prepare well, especially when it comes to pasta. But what I tell my students is to use the very best ingredients, particularly with the sauce. With pasta, I think that you sometimes have to oversalt the sauce in order to achieve the correct balance of flavors. (So if your sauce is a little on the salty side, don't worry.) Make sure you buy really fresh clams.

¼ cup extra virgin olive oil

2 cloves garlic, thinly sliced

¾ cup dry white wine (such as Sauvignon Blanc)

3 pounds Manila clams or other small clams, cleaned and scrubbed

Salt and freshly ground black pepper

1 pound fresh linguine

2 tablespoons chopped fresh flat-leaf parsley

2 Calabrian peppers, minced, or a pinch of crushed red pepper flakes

Fresh flat-leaf parsley sprigs as a garnish

Warm the olive oil in a large frying pan over medium heat. Add the garlic and cook for 1 minute. Increase the heat to high, add the white wine, and simmer until reduced by half, 1 to 2 minutes. Add the clams, cover, and cook until the shells open, 3 to 5 minutes. Discard any that don't open. Season with salt and pepper.

Bring a large pot of salted water to a boil. Add the pasta and cook until al dente, 3 to 4 minutes. Drain, and toss immediately with the clams, their sauce, the chopped parsley, and the Calabrian peppers or pepper flakes. Garnish with parsley sprigs and serve immediately.

Serves 6

Wine Suggestion: Chardonnay or Sauvignon Blanc

# moroccan grilled shrimp with fusilli

The Moroccans have a delicious sauce called *chermoula,* made with cilantro, parsley, lemon juice, garlic, cumin, turmeric, cayenne, and paprika. Here it flavors pasta with grilled shrimp. If you like this sauce, as I do, try serving it with chicken, shellfish, pork, veal, and even beef. These skewers can also be grilled on an outdoor grill.

6 bamboo skewers

Juice of 2 lemons plus 7 tablespoons fresh lemon juice

3 teaspoons ground cumin

1½ teaspoons sweet paprika

¾ teaspoon turmeric

⅓ teaspoon cayenne pepper

4 cloves garlic

½ yellow onion

½ cup chopped fresh cilantro

⅓ cup chopped fresh parsley

7 tablespoons extra virgin olive oil

Salt and freshly ground black pepper

1 pound medium-size fresh shrimp, peeled

¾ pound dried fusilli pasta

Fresh cilantro sprigs as a garnish

Lemon wedges as a garnish

In a shallow dish, soak the bamboo skewers in the juice of 2 lemons for 30 minutes.

In a blender or food processor, combine the cumin, paprika, turmeric, cayenne, garlic, onion, cilantro, parsley, 5 tablespoons of the olive oil, the 7 tablespoons lemon juice, and salt and pepper to taste. Puree until smooth. Reserve.

Thread the shrimp on the bamboo skewers. Brush the shrimp with the remaining 2 tablespoons olive oil.

Heat a ridged cast-iron grill pan over medium-high heat. Grill the shrimp until lightly golden, 2 to 3 minutes. Turn the skewers, season the shrimp with salt and pepper, and continue to cook until almost done, 2 to 3 minutes. Remove the shrimp from the skewers and set aside, covered with foil to keep warm.

Meanwhile, bring a large pot of salted water to a boil. Add the fusilli and cook until al dente, 8 to 12 minutes. Drain, and immediately toss with the sauce and the shrimp. Season to taste with salt and pepper. Serve immediately, garnished with cilantro sprigs and lemon wedges.

**Serves 6**

**Wine Suggestion: Sauvignon Blanc**

# horseradish-crusted salmon with dilled cucumbers with crème fraîche

I love horseradish; in fact, I grew up eating it because my father also loved it. When horseradish is heated, as in this dish, it loses some of its hotness but retains all of its flavor. I like to grate fresh horseradish in the food processor (but I warn you, don't put your nose in it to smell it). In this dish, inspired by my dear friend chef Gary Danko, the horseradish paste is spread on salmon medallions. When they're seared, the paste creates a piquant crust. Drizzle the cream sauce around the edges at serving time.

½ cup grated fresh horseradish (prepared horseradish may be substituted)

1 to 2 egg whites

Salt and freshly ground black pepper

2 pounds center-cut salmon fillet

Vegetable oil

1 cup fish stock or bottled clam juice

1 cup heavy cream

2 shallots, minced

1 cup dry white wine

1 recipe Dilled Cucumbers with Crème Fraîche (recipe follows)

Lemon wedges as a garnish

In a bowl, whisk together the horseradish and enough egg white to make a thick paste. Season with salt and pepper to taste.

Cut the salmon fillets into ¾-inch-wide strips. Roll up each strip, starting at the thick end. Secure each medallion with a bamboo skewer or a wooden toothpick.

Place 1 tablespoon of the horseradish paste on top of each salmon medallion, and spread it over the top of the medallion. Place the medallions on a plate and refrigerate until ready to cook.

Pour the fish stock into a small saucepan, place over high heat, and reduce to ½ cup. In another saucepan, reduce the heavy cream to ¾ cup. Add the cream to the

# chardonnay

The idea that fashions prevail in wine consumption runs counter to the notion that it's all about this or that year's perfect harvest. But so it is. Consider Chardonnay: During one decade (the 1980s), the total plantings of Chardonnay quadrupled worldwide. Nearly every winemaking country produces at least one Chardonnay, in climates as dissimilar as France, England, India, and Uruguay. It is easy to cultivate, produces high yields in a variety of climates, and is popular all over the world, especially America.

All this from its beginnings in the Burgundian heartland!

Chardonnay is the name of a white grape variety that is also used for the making of some Champagnes. When picked late, it has even produced creditable botrytized wines.

Some say its taste is hard to define. The Australian Wine Research Institute identified flavor components in Chardonnay that are found in vanilla, tropical fruits, peaches, tomatoes, tobacco, tea, and rose petals.

Arguably, much of the appeal of Chardonnay comes from the oaking, which some love, to which others are indifferent. But the oaking presents a problem for pairing with food, as heavily oaked Chardonnays have a relatively high alcohol content. The more that it is oaked, the less food-friendly it becomes. There is a definite trend, especially in Australia and Italy, toward less oaking, thus making Chardonnay more compatible with foods.

When it has little or no oak aging, Chardonnay pairs well with lighter dishes; when it has more oak aging, it is better with fuller-bodied dishes such as roast chicken, baked salmon, or even rich seafood.

fish stock. In a third saucepan, simmer the shallots in the white wine until 3 table-spoons remain when the solids are pressed. Strain. Add as much of the white wine reduction as needed to give the cream mixture a good flavor. Reserve the sauce.

Brush a nonstick sauté pan lightly with oil, and place it over medium-high heat. Add the salmon, horseradish side down, and reduce the heat to medium-low. Cook gently until a golden-brown crust is formed, 2 to 3 minutes. Turn the salmon over, and sauté gently until it is cooked through, 2 minutes. Season lightly with salt and pepper.

Divide the Dilled Cucumbers with Crème Fraîche evenly among eight dinner plates. Place the salmon medallions, horseradish crust up, on top of the cucumbers. Heat the cream sauce and drizzle around the edges, garnish with lemon wedges, and serve.

Serves 8

Wine Suggestion: Chardonnay or Viognier

## dilled cucumbers with crème fraîche

3 English (hothouse) cucumbers

2 teaspoons salt

2 tablespoons chopped fresh chives

2 tablespoons chopped fresh dill

¼ cup crème fraîche (recipe follows; also available at specialty stores)

2 teaspoons fresh lemon juice

Large fresh dill sprigs as a garnish

Peel the cucumbers in vertical stripes. Slice the cucumbers lengthwise, scoop out seeds, and cut into ¼-inch-thick diagonal slices. Toss the cucumbers and salt in a bowl. Transfer the cucumbers to a colander, and allow to drain for 15 minutes. Pat dry with paper towels.

In a bowl, toss together the cucumbers, chives, dill, crème fraîche, and lemon juice. Garnish with fresh dill sprigs.

Serves 8

# crème fraîche

1 cup heavy cream
2 tablespoons buttermilk, sour cream, or crème fraîche

Place the cream in a saucepan over medium heat. Heat to 100°F. Stir in the buttermilk, sour cream, or crème fraîche. Pour the mixture into a glass jar and cover. Let sit in a warm place, about 75°F, until the cream has thickened like sour cream, 12 to 14 hours. Cover and store in the refrigerator, where it will keep for 10 days.

Makes 1 cup

# crispy salmon with spiced lentils
# and herb salad

In the Moroccan marketplace, it is not unusual to find spices piled high by their vendors, who appreciate the role these intense colors and flavors have in the cooking of their country. In this dish, lentils cooked with an assortment of Moroccan spices set off a salmon fillet that's crisped by rapid cooking in olive oil.

6 pieces salmon fillet (about 2 pounds), skin removed

4 tablespoons extra virgin olive oil

1½ cups green or brown lentils

8 whole cloves, tied in a piece of cheesecloth

1 large red onion, minced

3 cloves garlic, minced

1½ teaspoons ground cumin

1½ teaspoons ground ginger

¾ teaspoon turmeric

¾ teaspoon sweet paprika

¼ teaspoon cayenne

3 peeled, seeded, chopped tomatoes, fresh or canned

1½ cups fish stock or bottled clam juice

⅓ cup chopped fresh parsley

⅓ cup chopped fresh cilantro

1 to 2 tablespoons fresh lemon juice

Salt and freshly ground black pepper

1 recipe Herb Salad (recipe follows)

6 lemon wedges as a garnish

Brush the salmon fillets with 1 tablespoon of the olive oil, place on a plate and cover with plastic wrap, and reserve in the refrigerator.

Sort the lentils and discard any stones or damaged lentils. Place the lentils and the

bag of cloves in a large saucepan and cover with water by 2 inches. Over high heat, bring to a boil. Turn the heat to medium-low and simmer, uncovered, until the lentils are almost tender, 15 to 25 minutes. Drain the lentils and discard the bag of cloves.

Heat the remaining 3 tablespoons olive oil in a large skillet, and cook the red onions over medium heat until soft, 7 minutes. Add the garlic, cumin, ginger, turmeric, paprika, and cayenne. Cook, uncovered, stirring occasionally, for 1 minute. Add the tomatoes and fish stock, and cook for 2 to 3 minutes. Then add the parsley, cilantro, and lentils, and cook, stirring occasionally, for 2 minutes. Season with the lemon juice and salt and pepper to taste. Keep warm.

Heat a sauté pan over medium heat. Sauté the salmon on one side until golden, 4 to 5 minutes. Turn the salmon, season with salt and pepper, and continue to cook until done, 3 to 4 minutes.

Spoon some of the warm lentils onto each plate. Place a piece of salmon in the middle, and garnish with the Herb Salad and lemon wedges.                    Serves 6

**Wine Suggestion: Sauvignon Blanc**

## herb salad

1½ tablespoons extra virgin olive oil

1 tablespoon fresh lemon juice

1 clove garlic, minced

Salt and freshly ground black pepper

¾ cup fresh flat-leaf parsley leaves

½ cup fresh cilantro leaves

½ cup small fresh basil leaves

¼ cup small fresh spearmint leaves

2 cups fresh arugula leaves

In a large bowl, whisk together the olive oil, lemon juice, garlic, and salt and pepper to taste.

Five minutes before serving, add the parsley, cilantro, basil, mint, arugula, and salt and pepper to taste. Toss together.                    Makes 4 cups

# hazelnut-crusted salmon with fennel salad

I like dishes that are "all-in-one": The salad or vegetable is there on the plate with the meat, fish, or chicken. The salad in this dish is composed of arugula, fennel, and oranges and goes on the plate first. It's topped with the salmon fillet, which is cooked until golden with a crust of hazelnuts and bread crumbs. This coating gives extra dimension to the flavor and is one of my favorite techniques for fish and chicken. A touch of hazelnut oil in the vinaigrette pulls the dish together.

1 cup shelled hazelnuts

½ cup dry bread crumbs

Salt and freshly ground black pepper

3 oranges

2 large bulbs fennel

1½ tablespoons hazelnut oil or other nut oil

3 tablespoons fresh orange juice

1½ tablespoons white wine vinegar

2 teaspoons grated orange zest

3 tablespoons extra virgin olive oil

1½ to 2 pounds fresh salmon fillets, cut into 6 serving pieces

2 tablespoons unsalted butter

3 cups very coarsely chopped arugula

½ cup green olives, pitted and chopped

Preheat the oven to 350°F.

Place the hazelnuts on a baking sheet and toast them in the oven until the skins crack and start to peel, 10 to 15 minutes (see page 273). Let the nuts cool a bit, and then rub off as much of the skin as possible in a rough kitchen towel. Place the hazelnuts in a food processor or blender, and grind until coarse. Add the bread crumbs and grind until finely grated. Season to taste with salt and pepper, and set aside.

Using a sharp knife, cut the tops and bottoms off the oranges to reveal the flesh.

Trim off all of the peel so that no white pith remains. Cut the oranges into sections, slicing between the membranes. Discard any seeds. Set the orange sections aside.

With a sharp knife, a mandoline, or an electric meat slicer, shave the fennel into paper-thin slices and reserve.

In a large bowl, whisk together the hazelnut oil, orange juice, vinegar, orange zest, and olive oil. Season with salt and pepper to taste. Divide the vinaigrette in half and reserve both portions.

Place the hazelnut mixture on a plate. Press each salmon fillet into the mixture to coat both sides.

Melt the butter in a large skillet over medium heat. Cook the salmon until golden on one side, 3 to 4 minutes. Turn the salmon and continue to cook until golden on the second side and cooked through, 3 to 4 minutes.

In the meantime, add the fennel, orange sections, arugula, and olives to one portion of the vinaigrette. Toss together, and line each plate with the salad. Top with the salmon, and drizzle the remaining vinaigrette over the salmon. Serve immediately.

**Serves 6**
**Wine Suggestion: Chardonnay**
**or Sauvignon Blanc**

# moroccan spice-dusted salmon with lemon mint yogurt

What a simple way to add flavor to a dish! Coat the fish (or chicken) with a combination of aromatic spices, inspired by the outdoor markets of Marrakech, and serve it with a yogurt sauce flavored with mint and citrus.

¼ cup fresh lime juice

2 tablespoons fresh lemon juice

½ cup fresh orange juice

1 teaspoon grated lime zest

½ teaspoon grated lemon zest

1 teaspoon grated orange zest

2 tablespoons chopped fresh mint

3 cups plain full-fat yogurt, drained in a cheesecloth-lined strainer for 12 hours

Salt and freshly ground black pepper

2 teaspoons whole cumin seeds

4 whole cardamom pods

2 teaspoons crushed whole coriander seeds

3 teaspoons whole fennel seeds

1 teaspoon salt

1 teaspoon freshly ground black pepper

2 tablespoons extra virgin olive oil

1½ to 2 pounds fresh salmon fillets, cut into 6 serving pieces

In a small saucepan, combine the lime, lemon, and orange juices with the lime, lemon, and orange zest. Bring to a boil over high heat. Simmer until the mixture is thick and syrupy and reduced to 2 tablespoons, 10 to 12 minutes. Combine the citrus syrup, mint, and drained yogurt. Season the sauce with salt and pepper to taste, and reserve.

Preheat the oven to 400°F.

Using a mortar and pestle or a spice grinder, grind the cumin, cardamom, coriander, and fennel seeds until crushed but not a fine dust. Stir in the salt and pepper. Spread the spice mixture on a plate, and dip one side of each salmon piece into the mixture to coat it heavily.

Warm the olive oil in a large heavy ovenproof frying pan over medium-high heat. Add the salmon, spice side down, and cook until the coating is golden and toasted, 2 to 3 minutes. Immediately place the pan in the oven, and bake for 4 minutes to finish cooking, turning halfway through. Place the salmon on a platter, crust side up, and serve immediately with the sauce.                                                    **Serves 6**

**Wine Suggestion: Chardonnay**

# grilled lamb with aromatic moroccan salts

This lamb dish is a version of one made by my friend Laurence Jossel of Chez Nous in San Francisco. It's served with Harissa Aïoli, a mayonnaise flavored with a spicy hot pepper condiment from Morocco. The mayonnaise can be homemade or store-bought; if you use store-bought, "doctor" it by adding 1 to 2 tablespoons extra virgin olive oil, some minced garlic, some fresh lemon juice, and salt to taste. Then add the harissa.

2 tablespoons grated orange zest

2 tablespoons grated lemon zest

2 teaspoons coarsely ground whole cumin seeds

1 teaspoon coarsely ground black peppercorns

½ teaspoon crushed red pepper flakes

2 tablespoons kosher salt

2 tablespoons extra virgin olive oil

1 leg of lamb (5 to 6 pounds), boned, excess fat removed, and butterflied

Fresh cilantro sprigs as a garnish

1 recipe Harissa Aïoli (recipe follows)

Preheat the oven to 200°F.

Place the orange and lemon zest on a baking sheet, and bake in the middle of the oven until dry, 20 to 30 minutes. Watch it very closely and remove from the oven immediately if done sooner. Remove from the oven and place in a small bowl. Add the cumin seeds, peppercorns, red pepper flakes, and kosher salt. Mix together.

Rub the olive oil all over the lamb. Rub half of the salt mixture all over the lamb. Let the lamb sit at room temperature for 10 to 20 minutes.

Heat a charcoal grill or the oven broiler.

Place the lamb 4 inches from the heat source on the grill rack or under the broiler. Cook until one side is golden, 15 minutes. Season well with salt and pepper. Turn the lamb and continue to cook until medium-rare (130°F to 135°F when tested with an instant-read thermometer), 15 minutes. Test by cutting into the thickest part. If it is

slightly pink inside, remove from the grill. Sprinkle the remaining salt mixture over the lamb, cover with foil, and let rest for 10 minutes.

Cut the lamb into thin slices and arrange them on a platter. Garnish with cilantro sprigs, and serve the Harissa Aïoli alongside.

**Serves 6 to 8**

**Wine Suggestion: Merlot or Cabernet Sauvignon**

## harissa aïoli

Harissa is a fiery-hot condiment used as a flavor enhancer in many dishes in Morocco, Algeria, and Tunisia. It can be made by hand or bought in a tube or in a small can in specialty food stores and even some grocery stores. It's made of dried hot red chile peppers, garlic, salt, and olive oil.

> 1 egg yolk
> 1 teaspoon Dijon mustard
> ½ cup pure olive oil
> ½ cup peanut, vegetable, corn, or safflower oil
> 2 to 3 cloves garlic, minced or mashed with a mortar and pestle
> Juice of 1 lemon
> 1 teaspoon harissa
> Salt and freshly ground black pepper
> 1 to 2 tablespoons warm water

In a small bowl, whisk the egg yolk, mustard, and 1 tablespoon of the olive oil together until an emulsion is formed. Combine the remaining olive oil and the peanut oil in a liquid measuring cup or small pitcher. Drop by drop, add the oil to the emulsion, whisking constantly. Continue to do this in a fine steady stream, whisking, until all of the oil has been added. Do not add the oil too quickly, and be sure that the emulsion is homogeneous before adding more oil. Add the garlic, lemon, and harissa. Season with salt and pepper to taste.

Before serving, add the warm water to the mayonnaise, whisking constantly, to thin it to a sauce consistency. This should be used the same day that it is made.

**Makes about 1 cup**

# lamb shanks, white beans, and tomatoes

My mother loves beans, and this happens to be one of her favorite dishes. After slow cooking with the vegetables, wine, and herbs, the meat just falls off the bone. The combination of flavors makes this a perfect dish for the fall or winter. You could also use veal shanks.

1½ cups (¾ pound) dried navy, white kidney, or cannellini beans

2 tablespoons extra virgin olive oil

6 lamb shanks (½ to ¾ pound each)

1 yellow onion, cut into ¼-inch dice

1 stalk celery, cut into ¼-inch dice

2 large carrots, cut into ¼-inch dice

6 cloves garlic, minced

1½ cups dry red wine (Cabernet Sauvignon, Chianti, Merlot)

2½ cups chicken stock

3 tablespoons tomato paste

1½ cups peeled, seeded, chopped tomatoes, fresh or canned

1 teaspoon chopped fresh thyme

1 bay leaf

Salt and freshly ground black pepper

1 tablespoon grated lemon zest

2 tablespoons chopped fresh flat-leaf parsley

Pick over the beans and discard any stones or damaged beans. Place them in a bowl, cover with plenty of water, and soak for 4 hours or overnight. Drain. Place the beans in a saucepan with enough fresh water to cover by 2 inches. Simmer, uncovered, until the skins begin to crack and the beans are tender, 45 to 60 minutes. Drain.

In a deep, heavy ovenproof casserole, heat the oil over medium heat. Add the lamb shanks and brown them on all sides, 10 to 12 minutes total. Remove from the pan and set aside. Add the onions, celery, and carrots to the pan and cook, uncovered, until the onions are soft, 10 minutes. Add the garlic and stir for 1 minute. Add the wine, chicken stock, tomato paste, tomatoes, thyme, bay leaf, and lamb shanks. Increase the heat and bring to a boil. Then reduce the heat to low and simmer, covered, until the shanks can be easily pierced with a skewer, 1½ to 2 hours. Add the beans, stir well, cover, and simmer slowly until the lamb begins to fall from the bone, 30 minutes. Season with salt and pepper to taste.

In a bowl, combine the lemon zest and parsley. Place the lamb and beans on serving plates, and garnish with the parsley mixture.                                    **Serves 6**

**Wine Suggestion: Barolo, Barbaresco, Chianti, Cabernet Sauvignon, or Merlot**

# the 38th parallel

Our maps of the world are so disjointed that it was several years of constant travel before I realized that all of my favorite places are bound together by a single line: the 38th parallel. It wraps around the globe connecting Sicily and Calabria in Italy, Murcia and Valencia in Spain, Athens in Greece, Izmir in Turkey, and, nearest to home, the California wine country in a near-continuous stream of sunlight and verdant land.

The countries that border the Mediterranean have much in common with the northern California valleys that have become so renowned for their wines. They share that dry heat that produces not just vineyards, but orchards of olive, fig, walnut, lemon, and apple trees; gardens of sweet tomatoes, garlic, red, green, and yellow bell peppers, squash, and eggplant. The air itself is scented with rosemary, basil, wild fennel, thyme, lavender, and mint.

These are the foods I love, the foods I relate to. Flatbread topped with walnuts and figs . . . tomatoes seasoned with basil and fruity olive oil . . . lamb skewered on fresh rosemary branches. But it's more than that.

The 38th parallel evokes an enchanted and unhurried way of living that winds and twists its way into the lives of its inhabitants like the vines on their trellises. Wherever I go, it is with me.

# braised leg of lamb with artichokes,
# with lemon and garlic–roasted potatoes

Forty cloves of garlic? Sounds like a lot. And how do you peel so many? Here's a trick: Soak them in a bowl of cold water for 10 minutes, and the skins will come right off. As the lamb cooks, the garlic just melts into the sauce. And with braising, the sauce is created right in the pan. That makes this one of my favorite dishes when I am entertaining. It uses a whole leg of lamb, but you should know that this isn't a lamb dish where the meat is served rare. Here the meat just falls off the bone.

> 6 medium-size or 18 small fresh artichokes
> Juice of 1 lemon
> 3 tablespoons olive oil
> 1 whole leg of lamb (5 to 6 pounds), bone-in
> Salt and freshly ground black pepper
> 2 yellow onions, minced
> 5 sprigs fresh thyme
> 1 cup chicken stock
> 1 cup dry white wine, such as Sauvignon Blanc
> 40 cloves garlic, peeled and crushed
> 1 recipe Lemon and Garlic-Roasted Potatoes (recipe follows)

Pare the artichokes (see page 237) and cut them in half or quarters. As you prepare them, place the artichokes in a bowl of water containing the lemon juice.

Warm 2 tablespoons of the olive oil in a large, heavy flameproof casserole over medium heat. Drain the artichokes and add them to the pan. Cook, stirring occasionally, until they just begin to become tender, 15 to 20 minutes. Remove with a slotted spoon and reserve.

In a large heavy pot, warm the remaining 1 tablespoon olive oil over medium heat. Season the lamb with salt and pepper. Add the lamb to the pan and cook, turning occasionally, until golden brown on all sides, 20 minutes. Add the onions and cook, stirring occasionally, until they are golden, 15 to 20 minutes. Reduce the heat to low and add the thyme, ¼ cup of the chicken stock, and ¼ cup of the wine. Cover and cook, turning the lamb occasionally, for 30 minutes. Add another ¼ cup stock and ¼ cup wine and continue to cook for 30 minutes. Repeat, adding the garlic as well as the stock and wine. Repeat one more time, for a total of 2 hours cooking time.

Remove the lamb from the pot, cover it with foil, and let it rest for 10 minutes. Remove and discard the thyme. Add the artichokes to the sauce in the pot and simmer until they are tender and the sauce has thickened slightly, 3 to 5 minutes.

Slice the lamb and arrange it on a platter. Spoon some of the artichoke sauce over the lamb. Pass the remaining sauce separately. Serve immediately with Lemon and Garlic–Roasted Potatoes.

**Serves 6 to 8**

**Wine Suggestion: Cabernet Sauvignon**

## paring an artichoke

With a serrated knife, cut through the artichoke crosswise (parallel to the base), just above the level of the choke or about halfway through the artichoke. Discard the top half of the artichoke.

Tear off the outer dark green leaves at the base of the artichoke, until you get to the light green leaves. Discard the dark green leaves.

With a paring knife, trim the torn edges of the base of the artichoke. Using a spoon, scrape out the hairy choke. Discard the parings and the hairy choke.

To prevent discoloration, place the artichoke hearts in a bowl of water containing the juice of 1 lemon until you are ready to use them.

# lemon and garlic–roasted potatoes

These potatoes are so good, you can serve them alongside any chicken, meat, or fish dish.

2 pounds russet potatoes, scrubbed but not peeled

¼ cup extra virgin olive oil

½ teaspoon salt

Freshly ground black pepper

Juice of 2 lemons

1 cup chicken stock

1 clove garlic, minced

1 tablespoon chopped fresh flat-leaf parsley

Zest of 1 lemon, finely chopped

Olive oil for frying

Preheat the oven to 375°F.

Cut the potatoes into wedges and place them in a bowl. Add the olive oil, salt, pepper to taste, and the lemon juice. Toss together.

Place the potatoes in a single layer in a baking pan, and drizzle with the oil/lemon mixture. Pour the stock into the pan.

Bake until the potatoes are golden brown and the stock has evaporated, 35 to 40 minutes. Allow the potatoes to cool.

In the meantime, chop the garlic and parsley together and mix with the lemon zest.

Heat 2 inches of olive oil to 375°F in a deep heavy saucepan. Add the potatoes and fry until golden and crispy, 1 to 1½ minutes. Toss with salt and pepper to taste, and place on a platter. Sprinkle with the parsley mixture, and serve.                Serves 6

# rolled veal with italian sausage and winter herbs, with crisp polenta triangles

Sometimes it seems that all of my favorite recipes are inspired by Italian dishes. This one is a great make-ahead company dish for the fall or winter. Veal scaloppini is stuffed and rolled, and then braised in a wine and balsamic-flavored tomato sauce. I like to sprinkle the finished veal rolls with Parmigiano and serve them with Crisp Polenta Triangles to mop up all the sauce.

## Veal

8 veal scallopine (about 1½ pounds), top or bottom round, cut across the grain

2 tablespoons extra virgin olive oil

1 small yellow onion, minced

2 cloves garlic, minced

3 tablespoons pine nuts

⅔ cup fresh bread crumbs

1 tablespoon chopped fresh sage

½ teaspoon chopped fresh thyme

½ teaspoon chopped fresh rosemary

Salt and freshly ground black pepper

10 ounces bulk sweet Italian sausage

## Sauce

2 tablespoons olive oil

2 yellow onions, chopped

½ cup red wine (Barolo, Cabernet Sauvignon, Côtes du Rhône)

2 tablespoons balsamic vinegar

Pinch of crushed red pepper flakes

1 teaspoon sugar

2 tablespoons tomato paste

½ teaspoon dried oregano

5 cups peeled, seeded, chopped tomatoes, fresh or canned

Salt and freshly ground black pepper

1 recipe Crisp Polenta Triangles (recipe follows)

½ cup grated Parmigiano-Reggiano for serving

Place each veal scallop between two pieces of plastic or waxed paper. With a meat mallet, pound the veal to slightly less than ¼-inch thickness.

Heat the extra virgin olive oil in a skillet over medium heat. Add the onions and cook, stirring occasionally, until soft, 7 minutes. Add the garlic and pine nuts and cook, stirring, for 2 minutes. Add the bread crumbs, sage, thyme, and rosemary, and continue to cook for 2 minutes. Season with salt and pepper to taste. Remove from heat, add the sausage, and mix well.

Place the veal pieces in a single layer on a work surface. Divide the stuffing evenly among the veal pieces. Spread the stuffing down the middle of each scallop, leaving the edges empty. Fold in the two long edges to partially cover the stuffing, and roll up the cutlet from the short end. Tie a piece of string around each roll as you would if you were wrapping a present. Set the veal rolls aside.

Prepare the sauce: Heat the olive oil in a large sauté pan over medium heat. Add the onions and cook until soft, 7 minutes. Add the red wine, balsamic vinegar, red pepper flakes, sugar, tomato paste, oregano, tomatoes, and salt and pepper to taste. Simmer until the sauce thickens slightly, 20 minutes. Remove the sauce from the heat and puree it in a blender or food processor until smooth. Return the pureed sauce to the pan, add the veal rolls, cover, and simmer until the rolls feel springy to the touch, 20 minutes.

Transfer the veal rolls to a warm platter, removing and discarding the strings. Pour the sauce over the rolls, and serve immediately with Crisp Polenta Triangles and grated Parmigiano.

Serves 6

Wine Suggestion: Cabernet Sauvignon, Barolo, or Chianti

# crisp polenta triangles

These polenta triangles are easy to prepare ahead of time. Just fry them at the last minute.

6 cups water

1 teaspoon salt

2 cups coarse polenta

½ cup grated Parmigiano-Reggiano cheese

4 tablespoons unsalted butter, room temperature

Salt and freshly ground black pepper

2 cups all-purpose flour

Olive oil for frying

Bring the water and salt to a boil in a large saucepan over high heat. Lower the heat to medium and slowly add the polenta, whisking constantly. Continue to whisk the mixture until it thickens, 3 to 5 minutes. Change to a wooden spoon and continue to simmer, stirring periodically, until the spoon stands upright in the polenta, 15 to 25 minutes. Add the Parmigiano and 2 tablespoons of the butter, and mix well. Season with salt and pepper to taste. Immediately spread the polenta in a buttered 9 x 9-inch baking pan. Smooth the top with a rubber spatula and let it cool in the refrigerator.

Cut the cooled polenta into 18 triangles. Put the flour in a shallow dish, and dredge the triangles in the flour, shaking off the excess.

Heat ½ inch of olive oil in a large deep frying pan to 375°F; a tiny piece of polenta should sizzle and turn golden on contact. Add a few of the polenta triangles and cook 1 to 2 minutes, turning occasionally, until golden on both sides. Drain on paper towels. Repeat until all the triangles have been cooked. Serves 6

# beef braised with zinfandel and winter vegetables

You can probably tell that I love braising; it's one of my favorite techniques for cooking meat, chicken, fish, or vegetables in the wintertime. The slow cooking process breaks down the fibers in meat and makes it tender. The technique is simple: First sauté the aromatics; next brown the meat; then add the liquid (broth, stock, or wine) to just the level of the meat; cover tightly; and then simmer very slowly either on the stove or in the oven until tender and flavorful. You'll love this one!

2 tablespoons olive oil

2 yellow onions, coarsely chopped

2 pounds beef stew meat, cut into 1½-inch pieces, excess fat removed

Salt and freshly ground black pepper

1 tablespoon all-purpose flour

8 fresh thyme sprigs, tied together with kitchen string

3 cloves garlic, chopped

2 bay leaves

2½ cups red Zinfandel wine

1½ cups peeled, seeded, chopped tomatoes, fresh or canned

3 cups beef or chicken stock

2 carrots, cut into 1½-inch lengths

2 parsnips, cut into 1½-inch lengths

2 turnips, cut into wedges

2 small rutabagas, cut into wedges

12 Brussels sprouts

Fresh thyme sprigs as a garnish

Preheat the oven to 375°F.

In a large, heavy flameproof casserole, warm the olive oil over medium heat. Add the onions and cook, stirring occasionally, until golden, 15 to 20 minutes. Remove the onions with a slotted spoon and reserve.

Increase the heat to medium-high, and add the beef in a single layer without crowding the pan. Season with salt and pepper to taste and cook, turning occasionally, until the beef is golden brown on all sides, 15 to 20 minutes. Pour off any excess fat from the pan. Return the pan to the heat and sprinkle the beef with the flour. Continue to turn the beef until the flour has turned golden brown. Return the onions to the pan, and add the thyme, garlic, and bay leaves. Stir together. Increase the heat to high, add the wine, and simmer, scraping up the cooked bits on the bottom of the pan. Cook until the wine has reduced by three-fourths, 10 to 12 minutes. Add the tomatoes and enough stock to cover the meat. Cover, and bring to a boil over high heat. Transfer the pan to the oven and braise until the meat is tender when pierced with a fork, about 1½ hours.

Remove the pan from the oven, remove the cover, and bring to a boil over high heat. Add the carrots, parsnips, turnips, rutabagas, and Brussels sprouts. Reduce the heat to medium-low and simmer until the vegetables are tender, 20 to 30 minutes. Using a slotted spoon, remove the beef and vegetables. Simmer the sauce until it thickens, 5 to 10 minutes. Return the beef and vegetables to the pan, and season with salt and pepper.

Ladle the stew into wide soup bowls, garnish with thyme sprigs, and serve immediately.

**Serves 6 to 8**

**Wine Suggestion: Zinfandel or Shiraz**

# desserts

zinfandel-poached pears with spiced zabaglione

blueberry brown butter tart

fig and walnut tartlets

apricot hazelnut tart

summer cherry and apricot galette with kirsch cream

three-minute almond cake with raspberries

del gallo fruit-filled summer cake

upside-down pear gingerbread

chocolate macadamia soufflé cake with soft cream

chocolate "brownie" with creamy mint anglaise

jean's best chocolate cake

orange citrus cake

orange and crystallized ginger biscotti

italian almond crumb cookie

polenta shortbread

scharffen berger meringue cookies

mango and pink grapefruit sorbet

strawberry rhubarb sorbet with strawberry sauce

caramelized pineapple with coconut sorbet

pineapple and meyer lemon sorbet

cinnamon apple sorbet

peach granita with sugared rose petals

ginger ice cream with chocolate-covered almonds

chocolate, cinnamon, and orange ice cream

yogurt and spiced walnuts drizzled with honey

# a state of grace

**I have said that living** in the wine country is like living in a state of grace. Why? I think it is because here there is something about the ever-present sun and the hillsides of vineyards that urges one to live life well and fully—to take more time, to be aware of the seasons, to set a beautiful table as many nights as one can, and sometimes to dine under the stars.

There is an art to living well, and it must be preserved. We must make many small celebrations of whatever catches our fancy. Dessert is the course that speaks loudest of pure pleasure. What other reason is there for it?

While I don't favor overly sweet desserts, I do believe that the meal should end on a special note. When I think about it, I suppose I like the texture of desserts more than their sweetness: a slice of shortbread that combines melt-in-your-mouth richness with the crunch of polenta; a mango sorbet that tingles with tangy sweetness; a creamy semolina custard with a warming fruit sauce. I love desserts that incorporate fruit! When I do make something gooey, I like it to be surprising—like a thin cake that looks for all the world like a brownie but tastes as light and rich as a soufflé. Or I like it to be steadfastly traditional—like Jean's Best Chocolate Cake.

And don't forget the cheese course! This delightful tradition provides a savory counterpoint between main course or salad and dessert—and it lets you linger even longer around the table. For many of us, a simple meal can end very happily with a bit of cheese and fruit. For gatherings of family and friends, however, the cheese course is a delicious teaser, heightening the anticipation of the sweet finale.

## composing a cheese course

Since my initial forays into the *fromageries* on my first trip to Paris, I have loved trying different cheeses. The cheese course, with its interesting variety, has always intrigued me and seems to be a great example of the whole being more than the sum of its parts. The composition of a great cheese course is part art—taste being subjective—and part intention. There are some rules I like to follow.

First, I limit myself to a total of three or four cheeses. And I try to pair cheeses by some rational design. For instance, I might put together a selection of all California cheeses or all farmstead cheeses. Another idea is to pick several of the blue cheeses from different countries: American Maytag Blue, English Stilton, French Roquefort, Italian Gorgonzola, Spanish Cabrales. And sometimes I'll put together a sampling of cheeses made from all the different types of milk—goat, sheep, and cow.

But my favorite way is to select cheeses that contrast different textures—such as a soft, fresh goat cheese with a farmhouse Cheddar or a hard aged Jack.

I try not to mix several strong cheeses together, and I encourage my guests to sample the cheeses in a sequence from mild to strong or soft to hard. I bring the cheeses to room temperature by removing them from the refrigerator at least three hours prior to serving. I like to serve them with different accompaniments, such as:

- Slices of fresh apples or pears, or small bunches of grapes
- Dried apricots and prunes (the sweetness is delicious with salty cheese)
- A cluster of dried raisins still on the vine
- Crackers, crusty bread, or walnut bread
- Toasted walnuts or pecans
- Quince paste

The cheese course can be served at various times: between the main and dessert courses, as the final course, or all by itself. This is where I grab a glass of red wine or port and just enjoy life in the wine country.

# farmstead cheeses

In recent years there has been an incredible resurgence of farmstead cheeses—cheeses that are made exclusively by hand with the milk of the cheesemaker's animals, whether goat, sheep, or cow. A new crop of cheesemakers are using traditional European cheesemaking methods to craft some of the most amazing cheeses and, really, to transform the image of American cheesemaking.

My first introduction to homemade cheeses, though, came in my grandmother's kitchen. Her farmer's cheese, the simplest of all to make, was my favorite. She'd start by setting some of the milk from the afternoon milking on the back burner of her stove—with no heat under it, just the residual warmth from the day's cooking and baking. Over the next couple of days, the milk would sour and curdle, forming curds and whey. She'd throw in a bit of salt and ladle the curds into a cheesecloth pouch about the size of a lunch bag. She'd tie a fat knot at one end of the pouch and hang it on a special nail over the sink and for hours the kitchen would be filled with a familiar ping . . . ping . . . ping as the whey dripped slowly away, leaving just the curds.

By the next morning, the pouch would be half its original size. My grandmother would lay it on the drainboard, cover it with a smooth piece of old barn wood, and weight that down with a large flat rock. Over the next few days, the cheese would take form and lose most of its moisture. On the fifth day, I'd help my grandmother peel away the cheesecloth to reveal the soft fresh cheese. I'll never forget how good it tasted on top of big slices of homemade rye bread, also from my grandmother's kitchen.

I think this return to farmstead and artisanal cheeses reflects our desire to get back to basics, and I couldn't be happier about it. These new cheesemakers are making art of nature's simplest bounty.

# wine and cheese pairing

Cheese influences the taste of wine much more then wine influences the flavor of cheese. Still, an auspicious pairing can bring out the best of each. Wine and cheese seem to naturally belong to one another, and actually each has very distinguishable chatacteristics to aid in your making a good or interesting match. Identify those characteristics (of acidity or intensity, for example) and then mirror or contrast them.

Wines and cheeses that share similar characteristics include the classic example of Sauvignon Blanc and fresh goat cheese; both the wine and the cheese have a high acid level, and so their flavors blend together easily. On the other end are low-acid white wines like an oaky Chardonnay paired with low-acid older cheeses. A light-intensity white like a Chenin Blanc would go well with a young, light-tasting cheese. And a higher-intensity wine like a Syrah would pair with a stronger cheese, like an aged Cheddar.

Another successful approach is to pair wines and cheeses with contrasting but complementary characteristics. A good example of this is a sweet dessert wine with a salty blue cheese; the sugar and salt are different but complementary flavors. An oaky California Chardonnay might pair well with a salty, nutty older cheese like a Gruyère, Emmentaler, or medium-aged Cheddar.

There is some feeling lately that red wines are harder to pair with cheese because of their tannins and their perhaps more complex flavors. Still, many red wines work well with cheese, including Cabernet Sauvignon, Syrah, and Merlot.

And finally, both Champagne and sparkling wine are good with soft-ripened cheeses like Camembert, Brie, or Parmesan, But so is a bold Cabernet Sauvignon—the qualities of those cheeses would soften the tannins in the wine.

So, much of this is subjective. Try new wines and cheeses, notice what you like, and soon you will be an expert in the art of wine and cheese pairing.

# summer bread pudding with berries

Bread pudding is a American classic and makes one of the best seasonal desserts when combined with lots of fresh berries. Be sure to use a good-quality bread, like brioche, homemade white bread, or other good quality white bread.

6 tablespoons unsalted butter, melted

10 slices (about ¾ pound) homemade white bread or brioche, crusts removed

1 cup fresh strawberries, hulled and halved

1 cup fresh raspberries

1 cup fresh blueberries

2½ cups half-and-half

3 tablespoons crème de cassis, or 1 tablespoon kirsch (optional)

½ cup sugar

½ vanilla bean, split lengthwise

2 eggs

4 egg yolks

Confectioner's sugar

Vanilla ice cream as a garnish

Preheat the broiler.

Reserving 1 tablespoon of the melted butter, brush the remaining butter over both sides of the bread. Toast until golden. Set the toast aside, and set the oven at 350°F.

In a bowl, gently mix the strawberries, raspberries, and blueberries. Spread one-third of the mixed berries on the bottom of a buttered 2-quart gratin dish. Top the berries with half of the toasted bread. Repeat the layers. Place the remaining berries on top, and brush them with the remaining 1 tablespoon melted butter.

In a saucepan, combine the half-and-half, crème de cassis, sugar, and vanilla bean. Heat the mixture over moderate heat, stirring occasionally, until the sugar has dissolved and the liquid is hot. Remove the vanilla bean and scrape the seeds into the hot milk mixture.

In a large bowl, whisk together the eggs and egg yolks until they are combined. Add the hot milk mixture in a slow steady stream, whisking constantly just until combined. Then pour the mixture carefully over the bread and berries.

Place the gratin dish in a larger pan, and pour enough boiling water into the larger pan to reach halfway up the sides of the gratin dish. Bake in the oven until the custard is just set, 20 to 30 minutes.

Sprinkle the top of the bread pudding with confectioner's sugar, and serve at room temperature with the ice cream. **Serves 6**

# lemon verbena flan with blueberries

Recently I've made a new herb discovery: lemon verbena. I grow it and find all kinds of uses for it. It is used in an elixir in Italy and to make tea in the south of France. You can find it at farmer's markets and specialty food stores, or you can grow it yourself. When steeped in milk for this custard, it imparts a scent that evokes the Mediterranean.

> 3 cups whole milk
> 1¾ cups sugar
> 30 fresh lemon verbena leaves, coarsely chopped
> 4 eggs
> 4 egg yolks
> ¼ teaspoon vanilla extract
> 1½ cups fresh blueberries

Combine the milk, ¾ cup of the sugar, and the lemon verbena in a saucepan over medium heat and bring almost to the boiling point. Remove from the heat and let sit, covered, for 2 hours.

In the meantime, melt the remaining 1 cup sugar in a heavy stainless-steel frying pan over medium-low heat, swirling the pan constantly until the sugar turns to a golden brown liquid and is just beginning to smoke, 4 to 5 minutes. Immediately remove the pan from the heat. Carefully pour the caramel into eight individual 5-ounce ramekins, turning the ramekins to coat the bottom and sides with the caramel.

Position the rack in the center of the oven, and preheat the oven to 350°F.

Scald the milk again. In a bowl, whisk together the eggs and egg yolks. Slowly add the hot milk to the eggs, a little at a time, whisking constantly. Strain the mixture into another bowl and add the vanilla. Pour the mixture into the caramel-lined ramekins, distributing it evenly.

Place the ramekins in a deep baking pan and fill the pan with enough hot water to reach halfway up the sides of the ramekins. Cover the pan tightly with foil, and bake until the custards are almost set but still slightly jiggly in the center, 35 to 45 minutes. Remove the ramekins from the hot water bath and allow to cool on a rack.

When you are ready to serve them, run a knife around the edge of each ramekin and turn the custard out onto the center of a plate, letting the excess sauce run over the custard. Garnish with the blueberries.                    **Serves 8**

# semolina custards with a sauce of poached fruits, riesling, thyme, and honey

Semolina is made from hard durum wheat that is ground more coarsely than regular wheat flour. I use it in pasta dough, gnocchi, and, as here, in a pudding served with a sauce of dried winter fruit. Sprigs of fresh thyme give the sauce a nice earthy flavor that marries well with the honey, wine, prunes, apricots, and figs. The sauce is served warm, making this a perfect comfort-food dessert for a cold evening.

**Sauce**
⅓ cup honey
1½ cups late harvest Riesling wine
½ cup water
2-inch strip of orange zest
4 sprigs fresh thyme
¼ pound pitted dried prunes
¼ pound pitted dried apricots
¼ pound dried Mission figs

**Custard**
4 cups whole milk
1 vanilla bean, split lengthwise and scraped
¾ cup sugar
½ cup semolina, sifted
4 tablespoons unsalted butter
1 teaspoon grated lemon zest
Pinch of salt
4 eggs, lightly beaten

In a large saucepan, bring the honey, wine, water, orange zest, and thyme to a boil over high heat. Add the prunes, apricots, and figs, and simmer, covered, until the fruit

is tender, 25 minutes. Remove the fruit with a slotted spoon. Increase the heat to medium-high and simmer until the syrup has reduced by one-third and thickened slightly, 5 to 10 minutes. Return the fruit to the pan and reserve.

Combine the milk and vanilla bean in a heavy saucepan. Heat to almost boiling over medium-high heat, and set aside for 20 minutes.

Remove the vanilla bean from the scalded milk, and stir in the sugar, semolina, butter, lemon zest, and salt. Stirring constantly, bring the mixture to a gentle boil. Reduce the heat to low and simmer, stirring constantly, for 5 minutes. Remove the pan from the heat. Place a piece of buttered baking parchment or waxed paper directly on top of the mixture (to prevent a skin from forming), and allow to cool. When the mixture is cool, add the eggs and stir together.

Butter 8 individual 5-ounce ramekins. Divide the custard mixture among the ramekins, distributing evenly. Position the oven rack in the center of the oven and preheat the oven to 350°F. Place the ramekins in a deep ovenproof baking pan and fill halfway with hot water. Cover tightly with foil and bake until a knife inserted into the center of the custards comes out clean, 30 to 40 minutes. Remove the ramekins from the hot water bath and cool on a rack.

To serve, run a knife around the edge of the ramekin and turn the custard out onto the center of a plate. Spoon the warm sauce around the custard and serve.     **Serves 8**

# double chocolate custard

This is a dessert to serve to somebody who *loves* chocolate! The recipe is a version of one by Lindsey Shere of Chez Panisse, and calls for an excellent-quality chocolate. Rich and delicious, these custards are best served after they have been out of the oven for at least three hours.

    4 ounces excellent-quality semisweet chocolate, chopped
    ½ ounce unsweetened chocolate
    ½ vanilla bean
    2 cups heavy cream
    3 tablespoons sugar
    6 egg yolks
    2 teaspoons Cognac or brandy

    Chocolate curls
    3 ounces bittersweet chocolate

Position the rack in the center of the oven, and preheat the oven to 350°F. Melt the two chocolates in the top of a small double boiler. As soon as they have melted, remove from the heat.

Split the vanilla bean and scrape the seeds from the pod. Discard the pod. Place the cream, sugar, and vanilla seeds in a saucepan and cook over medium-high heat until the mixture bubbles around the edges and the sugar has melted.

In a bowl, whisk the egg yolks and Cognac together. Slowly add the hot cream mixture, a little at a time, whisking constantly. Add the melted chocolate and stir together until well mixed. Pour the mixture into six individual 5-ounce ramekins, distributing it evenly.

Place the ramekins in a deep baking pan and add enough hot water to come halfway up the ramekins. Cover the pan tightly with foil, and bake until the custards are almost set but still slightly jiggly in the center, 30 to 40 minutes. Remove the ramekins from the hot water bath and allow to cool on a rack.

For the chocolate curls, melt the chocolate in the top of a double boiler. Place a rimless cookie sheet in the oven. When the sheet is very warm, use a pastry spatula to spread the melted chocolate evenly over about half of the sheet, to ⅛-inch thickness. Refrigerate the chocolate for 20 minutes.

Holding the blade of a pastry knife with both hands so it bends slightly, slide the knife under the chocolate, pulling it toward you at a 10° angle, to make curls. Place the curls on a parchment-lined baking sheet, and set aside until serving time.

To serve, place the custard cups on individual plates and garnish with the chocolate curls.                                                                 **Serves 6**

# caramelized coconut budino

I've never really liked coconut, but when a Tuscan friend of mine served this dish recently, I changed my mind. I'd been invited to breakfast and expected the usual breakfast fare. Instead she served two desserts, including this *budino*, or custard, that magically separates itself into three layers.

2½ cups very finely grated sweetened coconut

2 cups sugar

8 eggs

3 cups whole milk

3 tablespoons all-purpose flour

Preheat the oven to 325°F.

Place the coconut on a baking sheet and bake in the oven until light golden, tossing occasionally, 10 to 12 minutes. Let cool slightly. Place in a food processor and pulse until finely ground. Reserve. Increase oven temperature to 375°F.

In a large, heavy stainless-steel frying pan, melt 1 cup of the sugar over medium heat. Do not stir with a spoon; instead, swirl the pan to melt the sugar uniformly. Cook until the sugar starts to turn golden brown. Immediately remove the pan from the heat and pour the mixture into an 8-inch cake pan. Turn the cake pan to coat the bottom and sides with caramel. Set it aside.

Whisk the eggs together in a bowl. Add the remaining 1 cup sugar, the milk, coconut, and flour, and stir together until well mixed.

Pour the coconut mixture into the caramel-lined pan, and place in a larger pan. Pour boiling water into the larger pan to a depth of one inch. Bake in the oven until set and a skewer goes into the center and comes out clean, 55 to 65 minutes.

Remove the cake pan from the larger pan and let it sit for 10 minutes. Then invert the coconut *budino* onto a serving plate, and serve.                    Serves 8

# fig and raspberry clafouti

A *clafouti* is a country dessert that originated in the Limousin region of France but has since risen to national status. It consists basically of pancake batter that is poured over a layer of fresh fruit and then baked. Cherries are the traditional fruit of a *clafouti limousin,* but I have used figs and raspberries here, and you can use any kind of fruit you wish (try pears, plums, apples, or blackberries), depending upon the season.

10 fresh figs (about 1 pound), halved lengthwise

6 dried figs, thinly sliced

1 cup fresh raspberries

½ cup all-purpose flour

2¼ cups heavy cream

½ cup sugar

3 eggs

Pinch of salt

⅓ cup sliced almonds

2 teaspoons confectioner's sugar

¼ teaspoon vanilla extract

Preheat the oven to 400°F. Arrange the fresh figs, cut side up, in a buttered 2-quart baking or gratin dish. Sprinkle the dried figs and raspberries around and on top of the fresh figs. Set aside.

In a blender or food processor, combine the flour, 1¼ cups of the cream, the sugar, the eggs, and the salt. Process until well mixed, 30 seconds. Pour the batter over the fruit. Sprinkle the top with the sliced almonds. Bake in the middle of the oven until the top is golden and the batter is slightly firm to the touch, 25 to 30 minutes. Transfer the pan to a rack and let it cool for 15 minutes.

In the meantime, combine the remaining 1 cup cream with the confectioner's sugar and the vanilla, and whip until soft peaks form.

Spoon the clafouti onto individual plates, and serve with the whipped cream. **Serves 6**

# warm roasted nectarines with cherries and almonds

One of my favorite things is a dessert based on fruit. Simple and seasonal, there is just something so comforting about warm fruit with a scoop of vanilla ice cream or a dollop of whipped cream on top.

1 cup late harvest Riesling wine

¼ cup dried cherries

¼ cup blanched almonds

3 tablespoons unsalted butter, room temperature

1 egg yolk

2 tablespoons sugar

6 large fresh nectarines, preferably freestone

Vanilla ice cream or softly whipped cream

Warm the wine in a small saucepan over medium heat. Add the cherries and let sit, off the heat, for 20 minutes.

Meanwhile, preheat the oven to 350°F.

Place the almonds on a baking sheet and bake until light golden, 5 to 7 minutes. Remove them from the oven and chop into ¼-inch pieces. Let cool.

In a bowl, using a wooden spoon, beat together the butter, egg yolk, and sugar. Drain the cherries, reserving the wine, and add the cherries and the almonds to the butter mixture.

Slice each nectarine in half lengthwise and separate the halves by twisting them in opposite directions. Using a melon baller or a spoon, scoop out a bit more of the center so that you have a larger cavity for the stuffing. Place the nectarines in a single layer in a baking dish. Fill each cavity with 1 tablespoon of the cherry/almond/butter mixture. Pour the reserved wine into the baking dish.

Bake the nectarines until the filling is golden brown and the fruit is tender when pierced with a fork, 25 to 30 minutes. Remove the nectarines from the pan. If the juices on the bottom of the pan are thin, pour them into a small saucepan and reduce over high heat until syrupy.

Place 2 nectarines on each plate. Spoon the syrup around the nectarines, and serve with ice cream.                                                                **Serves 6**

# honey-poached plums with mascarpone

Plums are originally from China, but of course they are now grown widely, especially in California. This simple summertime dessert can be made with any of the many varieties of plums, from the dark red-skinned "Santa Rosa" to the blue-skinned "President." The poached plums are served warm, with honey-flavored mascarpone that melts on top. Use a moderately priced tawny port, or substitute any fruity red wine (such as Zinfandel, Pinot Noir, or Merlot). If you use the red wine, increase the honey in the poaching liquid to 1½ cups.

> 3 cups tawny port
> 1 cup plus 2 tablespoons honey
> 3 whole cloves
> 1 cinnamon stick, 3 inches long
> 2½ pounds firm ripe plums
> ½ cup mascarpone cheese
> 1 tablespoon whole milk

Place the port, 1 cup of the honey, cloves, and cinnamon stick in a saucepan and bring to a boil over medium-high heat. Reduce the heat to low and simmer for 5 minutes.

In the meantime, halve and pit the plums.

Increase the heat to high, add the plums to the pan, and bring to a boil. Then reduce the heat to low and simmer until the plums can be easily pierced with a knife but still hold their shape, 4 to 5 minutes. Using a slotted spoon, transfer the plums to a bowl. Return the pan to the heat and simmer until the liquid has reduced by half and is just beginning to thicken, 10 minutes. Remove and discard the cloves and cinnamon sticks. Pour the liquid over the plums, and reserve.

In a small bowl, stir together the mascarpone, milk, and remaining 2 tablespoons honey.

To serve, warm the plums and their liquid in a saucepan over medium heat. Spoon the plums into individual bowls, and top each serving with a dollop of mascarpone.

**Serves 6**

# zinfandel-poached pears
# with spiced zabaglione

This zabaglione was inspired by a trip to Sicily. Although zabaglione is traditionally made with just eggs, sugar, and Marsala, I've added raisins, cloves, and cinnamon. It makes a perfect winter dessert.

**Pears**

4 cups red Zinfandel wine

8 cinnamon sticks, 3 inches long

16 whole cloves, tied in a piece of cheesecloth

1½ cups sugar

6 Bosc pears, peeled, quartered, and cored

**Zabaglione**

⅓ cup golden raisins

½ cup sweet Marsala wine

4 egg yolks

¼ cup sugar

¼ teaspoon ground cinnamon

¼ teaspoon ground cloves

Combine the Zinfandel, cinnamon sticks, bag of cloves, and sugar in a saucepan over medium heat, and bring to a boil. Add the pears and simmer until they can be easily pierced with a fork, 20 to 40 minutes (depending upon the ripeness of the pears). Remove and discard the bag of cloves and the cinnamon sticks. Reserve the pears in the poaching liquid.

Prepare the zabaglione: Place the raisins and Marsala in a small saucepan. Bring to a boil, and immediately remove from the heat. Let steep until cool.

Strain the raisins, reserving the Marsala. Bring a saucepan of water to a simmer.

Whisk the egg yolks and sugar together in a stainless-steel bowl until light and foamy. With a large balloon whisk, whisk in the reserved Marsala. Set the bowl over the pan of barely simmering water. Don't let the water touch the bottom of the bowl. Whisk constantly until the mixture is thick, feels hot to the touch, and holds a shape and there is no liquid left at the bottom of the bowl, 3 to 5 minutes. Add the raisins, cinnamon, and cloves to the zabaglione and whisk together.

Warm the pears over medium heat. Using a slotted spoon, transfer the pears to a serving dish. Spoon the zabaglione over the pears, and serve immediately.    **Serves 6**

# blueberry brown butter tart

Blueberries crown this beautiful and great-tasting tart. Brown butter is called *beurre noisette*, "hazelnut butter," in French. The butter is cooked until it turns a light hazelnut brown and imparts a nutty aroma. The flavor marries particularly well with fruit—blueberries as well as other varieties.

3 eggs

1¼ cups sugar

1 tablespoon grated lemon zest

1 teaspoon vanilla extract

¼ cup all-purpose flour, sifted

12 tablespoons (1½ sticks) unsalted butter

1 prebaked Sweet Short Crust Tart Shell (recipe follows)

1 cup fresh blueberries

Topping

2 cups water

1½ cups sugar

2½ cups fresh blueberries

½ cup confectioner's sugar

In a large bowl, whisk the eggs, sugar, lemon zest, and vanilla extract until combined. Sift the flour over the top and mix well. Set aside.

In a small saucepan over medium-high heat, melt the butter until it is foamy. Continue to heat the butter until the foam begins to subside and the butter begins to turn brown, just starts to smoke, and gives off a nutty aroma. Whisking continuously, pour the hot butter in a steady stream into the egg mixture, combining well. Let the mixture cool to room temperature.

Preheat the oven to 350°F.

Sprinkle the 1 cup blueberries evenly over the bottom of the prebaked tart shell. Pour the brown butter mixture over the blueberries, filling the shell two-thirds full. Bake until the filling is firm to the touch, 45 to 55 minutes. Let the tart cool completely.

For the topping, combine the water and sugar in a saucepan, and bring to a boil over medium heat. Boil for 30 seconds. Place the blueberries in a colander set over a bowl. Pour the syrup over the berries, coating them completely and allowing the excess to run into the bowl. Shake the colander to remove the excess syrup. Mound the berries onto the cooled tart, covering the entire top.

Just before serving, sift the confectioner's sugar over the top.          Serves 8

## sweet short crust tart shell

1¼ cups all-purpose flour

1 tablespoon sugar

Pinch of salt

1 teaspoon grated lemon zest

10 tablespoons (1¼ sticks) unsalted butter, out of the refrigerator for 15 minutes,
   cut into small pieces

Up to 1 tablespoon water, room temperature

In a food processor, mix the flour, sugar, and salt with a few pulses. Add the lemon zest and butter, and pulse until the mixture resembles cornmeal. Add the water as needed until the dough just holds together in a ball. Remove the dough from the processor and flatten it into a 6-inch-diameter cake. Wrap it in plastic wrap and refrigerate for 30 minutes.

Preheat the oven to 400°F.

Press the pastry evenly onto the bottom and sides of a 9-inch tart pan. Chill the tart shell in the freezer for 30 minutes.

Line the pastry with baking parchment, and scatter 1 cup of dried beans or pie weights onto the parchment. Bake the tart shell until the top edges are light golden, 10 to 15 minutes. Remove the parchment and weights, reduce the heat to 375°F, and continue to bake until the shell is light golden, 15 to 20 minutes.

**Makes one 9-inch tart shell**

# fig and walnut tartlets

Figs are an ancient fruit, dating from at least 2000 B.C. They were brought to the New World by the Spanish in the 16th century. In the mid to late 1700s, the first fig trees were planted by the Franciscans as they established their missions in what would become California (hence the name "Mission" fig). The first trees were planted in San Diego, and then at other missions as the Franciscans traveled northward to Sonoma. For these tartlets, I've paired fresh figs with walnuts and flavored them with brandy and orange zest. Serve them hot or at room temperature, with soft whipped cream or vanilla ice cream.

> 1 cup walnut halves
>
> ⅓ cup confectioner's sugar
>
> 2 tablespoons all-purpose flour
>
> 1½ tablespoons unsalted butter
>
> 1 large egg
>
> 1 tablespoon brandy or Cognac
>
> 1 teaspoon grated orange zest
>
> 4 fresh figs, cut into ½-inch dice
>
> 1 recipe Sweet Short Crust dough (see page 270), unbaked
>
> 5 fresh figs, cut into ¼-inch-thick slices
>
> 1 cup heavy cream
>
> 1½ tablespoons sifted confectioner's sugar
>
> 1 teaspoon vanilla extract
>
> Confectioner's sugar as a garnish

Preheat the oven to 350°F.

Place the walnuts on a baking sheet and bake until lightly golden, 5 to 7 minutes. Remove, and let cool for 15 minutes. Increase the oven heat to 400°F.

In a food processor, process the walnuts and half of the confectioner's sugar until fine, 30 to 60 seconds. Sift the remaining confectioner's sugar and the flour on top, and pulse several times until well mixed. Add the butter, egg, brandy, and orange zest and pulse until well mixed. Transfer the mixture to a bowl, add the diced figs, and stir together carefully. Set aside.

Divide the short crust dough into 8 equal pieces. With your fingertips and the palm of your hand, press the pastry into eight individual 3-inch tart pans, forming an even layer on the bottom and building up the sides slightly. (Alternatively, the dough can be rolled out on a floured surface to ⅛-inch thickness and fitted into the pans.) Chill the shells in the freezer for 15 minutes. (This can be done up to a week ahead of time; wrap the shells in plastic wrap and store them in the freezer.)

Line the pastry shells with baking parchment or aluminum foil, and scatter dried beans or pie weights onto the parchment. Place the tart pans on a baking sheet, and bake until the top edges are light golden, 10 to 12 minutes. Remove the parchment and weights, reduce the heat to 375°F, and continue to bake until the shells are light golden, 5 to 10 minutes.

Remove the pans from the oven, and fill them evenly with the reserved fig mixture. Top with the sliced figs, and return to the oven. Bake until the filling is set and the tops are golden, 35 minutes.

In the meantime, whip the cream with a whisk or an electric mixer until soft peaks form. Flavor the whipped cream with the sifted confectioner's sugar and the vanilla extract.

Remove the tarts from the oven and serve immediately, dusted with confectioner's sugar and with the whipped cream on the side. Serves 8

# apricot hazelnut tart

Hazelnuts have a great earthy flavor that is wonderful when paired with apricots, as in this dish. Also called filberts, hazelnuts are now grown in Oregon and Washington. Just sixty years ago, they were all imported from Italy, Spain, France, or Turkey—countries that are still the leading producers of these wild nuts. When you cook with hazelnuts, you have to remove the bitter brown skin. Do this by toasting them in a 350°F oven for 10 to 15 minutes, until the skin begins to flake; then rub them vigorously in a rough kitchen towel to remove as much of the skin as possible.

Pastry
1 cup all-purpose flour
¼ teaspoon salt
8 tablespoons (1 stick) unsalted butter, room temperature
¼ pound cream cheese, room temperature

Filling
4 tablespoons unsalted butter, room temperature
½ cup sugar
2 eggs
1 teaspoon grated lemon zest
1½ cups shelled hazelnuts, toasted and peeled (see headnote), finely ground
3 tablespoons apricot jam, heated and strained
1 cup heavy cream
Confectioner's sugar

Prepare the dough: Place the flour and salt in a large bowl. Cut the butter and cream cheese into 1-inch pieces. With your hands, rub the flour, butter, and cream cheese together until the mixture resembles coarse meal. Gather the dough into a ball, wrap it in plastic wrap, and let it rest at room temperature for 30 minutes.

In the meantime, in an electric mixer, mix together the butter, sugar, eggs, lemon zest, and ground hazelnuts. Set aside.

Dust a work surface and a rolling pin with flour. Roll the dough out to fit into an 11-inch tart pan. Fit it into the pan, crimp the edges, and chill in refrigerator for 30 minutes.

Preheat the oven to 375°F.

Spread the strained apricot jam over the bottom of the pastry shell, and then pour the filling on top. Bake on the bottom shelf of the oven until the top is golden and the filling is set, 30 minutes. Let cool to room temperature.

While the tart is cooling, whip the cream until soft peaks form. Flavor it with confectioner's sugar to taste.

When the tart has cooled, dust the top lightly with confectioner's sugar. Serve wedges of the tart with the whipped cream on the side.          **Serves 8**

# summer cherry and apricot galette with kirsch cream

For me, the best desserts come right out of the orchard. Cherries in May; the stone fruits and berries of summertime; pears and apples in the fall; and winter lemons, blood oranges, and limes. A galette, which is simply a thin open-face tart, can be the perfect host for summer cherries and apricots, or whatever happens to be in season.

1½ cups all-purpose flour, chilled in the freezer for 1 hour

Pinch of salt

9 tablespoons sugar

9 tablespoons unsalted butter, cut into ½-inch dice, chilled in the freezer for 1 hour

⅓ to ½ cup ice water

3 tablespoons ground blanched almonds

1 pound fresh apricots, pitted and cut into eighths

¾ pound fresh cherries, pitted

1 cup heavy cream

1 tablespoon confectioner's sugar

2 tablespoons kirsch

Place the flour, salt, and 2 tablespoons of the sugar on a work surface. Stir together. With a pastry scraper, cut the butter into the flour until half the mixture is the size of peas and the rest a little smaller. (Alternatively, this can be done in a food processor, pulsing several times. Turn the mixture onto the work surface to add the water.) Add the ice water, a little at a time, just until the mixture holds together. Roll the dough out on a well-floured surface to form a 14-inch circle, and place it in a jelly roll pan.

Combine 3 tablespoons of the sugar with the ground almonds, and sprinkle this over the center of the dough, leaving a 3-inch border. Place the pastry in the refrigerator and chill 30 minutes.

Preheat the oven to 375°F.

In a large bowl, toss together the apricots, cherries, and remaining 4 tablespoons sugar.

Remove the pastry from the refrigerator. Spread the fruit over the center of the pastry, leaving a 3-inch border. Fold the uncovered edge up and over the fruit, pleating it to make it fit. There will be an open space revealing the fruit. Bake until golden brown, 35 to 40 minutes.

In the meantime, combine the cream, confectioner's sugar, and kirsch in a bowl, and whip until soft peaks form.

Remove the galette from the oven and let it cool for 5 minutes. Then slide it off the pan and onto a serving plate. Cut the galette into wedges, and serve with the kirsch cream on the side.

**Serves 6 to 8**

# three-minute almond cake
# with raspberries

Need a quick dessert? Just throw everything into the food processor and it's ready to bake in three minutes! You'll also please any almond-lover with this cake. Serve it with raspberry sherbet, and spoon the sauce over the sherbet.

> 1¼ cups sugar
>
> 7 ounces almond paste
>
> 1¼ cups (2½ sticks) unsalted butter, room temperature
>
> 6 eggs, room temperature
>
> 1 cup all-purpose flour
>
> 1½ teaspoons baking powder
>
> ¼ teaspoon salt
>
> 3 cups fresh raspberries
>
> ¼ cup crème de cassis
>
> Sugar (optional)
>
> Raspberry sherbet
>
> Confectioner's sugar as a garnish

Preheat the oven to 325°F. Butter and flour a 13 x 9-inch baking pan.

In a food processor, cream the sugar and almond paste until well mixed. Add the butter and process until light and fluffy. Beat in the eggs, one at a time, pulsing after each addition. In a mixing bowl, sift the flour, baking powder, and salt together. Add the dry ingredients to the egg mixture and process just until thoroughly blended.

Turn the batter into the prepared pan, smoothing the top evenly. Bake until a toothpick inserted in the center comes out clean and the center feels springy when you press it gently, 30 to 40 minutes. Cool on a rack for 20 minutes. Remove from the pan.

Using a 3-inch round cutter, cut out as many circles of cake as possible. Cut each one in half to form 2 half-moons.

Puree 1½ cups of the raspberries in a blender until smooth. Strain, and place in a bowl with the remaining 1½ cup raspberries, the crème de cassis, and sugar to taste if needed.

To serve, place 2 pieces of cake on each plate. Place a scoop of sherbet next to the cake. Spoon the raspberry sauce over the sherbet, and dust the top with confectioner's sugar.

**Serves 6 to 8**

# del gallo fruit-filled summer cake

Laconda del Gallo, a small Umbrian inn, is the source of this cake. I was there recently with a group of students for a week of study. The chef went out into the orchard to pick all kinds of fruit, and this is what he came up with. You can use any kind of summer fruit, including an assortment of berries.

½ cup fresh cherries, pitted

½ cup fresh strawberries, hulled and cut in half

2 fresh peaches or nectarines, peeled, halved, pitted, and cut into wedges (1 cup)

1½ cups cake flour

¾ teaspoon baking powder

½ teaspoon baking soda

¼ teaspoon salt

12 tablespoons (1½ sticks) unsalted butter, room temperature

½ cup sugar

3 eggs

1 tablespoon rum

2 teaspoons grated lime zest

½ cup plain yogurt

1 cup heavy cream

1 tablespoon confectioner's sugar

Preheat the oven to 350°F.

Oil a 9 x 9-inch baking pan.

Place the cherries, strawberries, and peaches in a bowl and toss gently together.

Sift the cake flour, baking powder, baking soda, and salt together in a bowl, and re-serve.

In an electric mixer, cream the butter until light and creamy, 2 minutes. Add the sugar and continue mixing until light and fluffy, 2 minutes. In a separate bowl, whisk together the eggs, rum, and lime zest. Gradually add this mixture to the creamed butter/sugar mixture. Add the dry ingredients in three batches, mixing after each addition. Add the yogurt and stir just until mixed.

Pour half of the batter into the prepared pan. Spread the fruit evenly over the top. Pour the remaining batter over the fruit. Bake until a toothpick inserted into the center comes out clean, 30 minutes.

Meanwhile, whip the cream and confectioner's sugar in a bowl until soft peaks form.

Remove the cake from the oven and cool it in the pan. Cut it into squares, and serve warm or at room temperature, with the whipped cream alongside.  **Serves 9**

# upside-down pear gingerbread

Every New England child (including myself) learns to love gingerbread. This one is unusual, and is beautiful when served on a square plate for a special autumn dinner, or even Thanksgiving or Christmas.

1 cup (2 sticks) plus 6 tablespoons unsalted butter

⅓ cup plus 1 cup plus 2 tablespoons (or 18 T) light brown sugar, packed

2 Bosc pears, peeled, quartered, cored, and thinly sliced

3 eggs

½ cup molasses

3 cups all-purpose flour

2 tablespoons ground ginger

1 tablespoon ground cinnamon

1¼ tablespoon baking soda

¾ teaspoon freshly grated nutmeg

¾ teaspoon ground cloves

Pinch of salt

1¼ cups boiling water

1 cup heavy cream

¼ teaspoon vanilla extract

Confectioner's sugar

Preheat the oven to 350°F.

Place a 9-inch square flameproof cake pan over medium heat. Heat 4 tablespoons of the butter and the ⅓ cup brown sugar in the pan just until the sugar melts. Then add the pear slices, arranging them in a decorative pattern.

In an electric mixer, cream the remaining 1 cup plus 2 tablespoons butter and the remaining 1 cup plus 2 tablespoons brown sugar until light. Beat in the eggs and molasses. In another bowl, sift together the flour, ginger, cinnamon, baking soda, nutmeg, cloves, and salt. Fold the dry mixture into the creamed mixture, along with the boiling water, stirring just until all the ingredients are mixed. Do not overmix.

Spoon the batter over the pears, and bake in the oven until springy to the touch, 30 to 40 minutes. Let the cake cool for 5 minutes.

Meanwhile, whip the cream until soft peaks form. Flavor it with the vanilla and confectioner's sugar to taste.

Carefully invert the cake onto a serving plate. Cut the cake into 9 squares. Place a square on each plate, and serve with the whipped cream on the side.          **Serves 9**

# chocolate macadamia soufflé cake
# with soft cream

Want to make a cake day ahead of time and still have it taste fabulous? This one is made with very little flour, so it is very moist. The butter and chocolate make it very rich and chocolate-y without being too sweet. If you don't ice it until you are ready to use it, it can keep for three to four days. Don't refrigerate or freeze it; just cover it with foil while it's still in the pan.

1 cup (2 sticks) unsalted butter

9 ounces excellent-quality bittersweet chocolate, finely chopped

6 eggs, separated

¾ cup sugar

6 tablespoons light brown sugar

3 tablespoons ground macadamia nuts

6 tablespoons all-purpose flour

½ teaspoon cream of tartar

1 cup heavy cream, chilled

¼ teaspoon vanilla extract

1 tablespoon confectioner's sugar

Confectioner's sugar as a garnish

Butter the sides and bottom of a 9-inch springform pan, and line the bottom with baking parchment. Dust with flour and tap out the excess.

Preheat the oven to 350° F.

In the top of a double boiler, heat the butter and chocolate just until melted and smooth. Set aside and keep warm.

In a bowl, beat the egg yolks, sugar, and brown sugar just until mixed. Whisk the egg mixture into the warm chocolate. Combine the nuts and flour in a food processor and process until fine. Stir into the chocolate mixture.

Beat the egg whites and the cream of tartar in a large bowl until stiff peaks form. Carefully fold the whites into the chocolate mixture. Pour the batter into the prepared pan, and bake until the cake is completely set around the sides but still has a soft, creamy center about 6 inches across, 35 to 45 minutes. The cake should jiggle just slightly when you shake the pan gently. Cool the cake in the pan.

Just before serving, combine the cream, vanilla, and confectioner's sugar in a bowl and whip until soft peaks form. Dust the top of the cake with confectioner's sugar. Cut the cake into wedges, and serve a dollop of the whipped cream on the side.

Serves 8 to 10

# chocolate "brownie" with creamy mint anglaise

I think of these as deceptive brownies because while they look like brownies, they are actually more like a light soufflé cake. They contain no flour—just chocolate, butter, eggs, and sugar. Like so many of my favorite desserts, they were inspired by ones at Chez Panisse. Serve them with Creamy Mint Anglaise.

> 1 cup (2 sticks) unsalted butter
> 7½ ounces bittersweet chocolate
> 7½ ounces semisweet chocolate
> 6 eggs, separated
> 1⅛ cups sugar
> Confectioner's sugar
> 1 recipe Creamy Mint Anglaise (recipe follows)

Preheat the oven to 350°F.

Butter the sides and bottom of a 9 x 13-inch baking pan. Line the bottom with baking parchment and flour the pan lightly.

Melt the butter in a large heavy saucepan. Chop both chocolates coarsely and combine them with the butter in a double boiler. Stir constantly over low heat until just melted and smooth; be careful not to overheat, or the chocolate will turn grainy. It should not get much hotter than 115°F.

In a bowl, beat the egg yolks with 9 tablespoons of the sugar until a ribbon forms when you lift the beaters. Beat the chocolate mixture into the egg mixture.

Warm the egg whites slightly by swirling them in a stainless-steel bowl above a gas flame or over hot water. Beat the whites until they form stiff peaks. Add the remaining 9 tablespoons sugar and continue to beat, incorporating the sugar completely without deflating the whites. Spread the egg whites over the chocolate mixture and fold them together quickly without deflating the whites. Pour into the prepared pan

and bake for 30 to 35 minutes. The "brownie" is done when it has risen around the edges and cracked slightly.

While it is still warm, turn the "brownie" out of the pan onto a rack. Remove the parchment while it is still warm. Turn the "brownie" over, trim the edges, and cut it into squares.

Decorate the top with a sprinkling of confectioner's sugar, and serve with the Creamy Mint Anglaise alongside.                                                          Serves 12

## creamy mint anglaise

12 large sprigs fresh mint

3 cups whole milk

5 tablespoons sugar

½ vanilla bean, split and scraped

6 egg yolks

With the back of a chef's knife, bruise the mint stems and leaves well.

Combine the milk, sugar, vanilla bean, and the mint in a saucepan over medium heat. When the mixture bubbles around the edges, remove the pan from the heat and set aside for 1 hour.

In a large bowl, whisk the egg yolks to break them up, but don't make them foam.

Scald the milk mixture again, and then strain it. Discard the mint. Whisk a little of the hot milk into the egg yolks to warm them. Slowly add the remaining hot milk to the eggs, whisking constantly. Return the mixture to the pan and place over medium heat. Cook the custard, stirring constantly, until it coats the back of a spoon, 3 to 8 minutes. Test it by drawing your finger across the back of the spoon: If it leaves a trail in the custard, the custard has cooked to the right point. (It can also be tested with a thermometer: It should register 170°F.) Immediately strain the custard into a bowl. Chill until ready to serve.                                              Makes about 3½ cups

# jean's best chocolate cake

My Mom, Jean Tenanes, has cooked professionally her whole life and is a great pastry chef. This moist cake is reminiscent of the great chocolate cakes she made for us when we were kids.

Cake

1 cup boiling water

4 ounces excellent-quality unsweetened chocolate, chopped

8 tablespoons (1 stick) unsalted butter

2 eggs

2 cups sugar

2 teaspoons vanilla extract

2½ cups all-purpose flour

2 teaspoons baking powder

2 teaspoons baking soda

½ teaspoon salt

1 cup freshly brewed hot coffee

Frosting

8 tablespoons (1 stick) unsalted butter, room temperature

2 tablespoons milk or cream

1⅓ cups confectioner's sugar, sifted

2 ounces excellent-quality unsweetened chocolate, melted

1 teaspoon vanilla extract

Preheat the oven to 350°F. Butter and flour two deep 8-inch cake pans, tapping out the excess flour.

Place the boiling water, chopped chocolate, and butter in the top of a double boiler over medium-high heat. Stir until the mixture is melted and smooth. Remove from the heat.

With an electric mixer, beat the eggs in a bowl until foamy, 15 seconds. Add the

sugar and vanilla and continue to mix until creamy, 15 seconds. Stir in the chocolate mixture.

In another bowl, sift the flour, baking powder, baking soda, and salt together. Add this to the chocolate mixture and mix until almost incorporated. Add the hot coffee and mix until well combined, but do not overmix. Pour the batter into the prepared pans. Bake until a toothpick inserted in the center comes out clean and the cake is pulling away from the sides of the pan, 25 to 30 minutes.

In the meantime, make the frosting: Place the butter, milk, confectioner's sugar, melted chocolate, and vanilla in the bowl of an electric mixer. Beat until smooth, about 1 minute.

When the cake is done, remove it from the oven and let it cool on a wire rack for 20 minutes. Then run a knife around the edges of the pan, and invert the cake onto the rack. Allow it to cool completely.

Spread half of the frosting onto one of the cake layers. Top with the other cake layer, and frost the top.

To serve, cut into wedges.                               Serves 8 to 10

# orange citrus cake

I've always thought of desserts flavored with lemon and orange as "old people's desserts." I guess I'm getting older (well, maybe more mature) because I now love them. If you love orange, you'll love this one.

2½ cups all-purpose flour

2½ teaspoons baking powder

½ teaspoon salt

12 tablespoons (1½ sticks) unsalted butter

1¾ cups sugar

1½ teaspoons vanilla extract

2 tablespoons grated orange zest

2 eggs

1 cup fresh orange juice

¼ cup milk

1 recipe Orange Buttercream (recipe follows)

Preheat the oven to 350°F. Oil and lightly flour two 8 x 1½-inch round baking pans, or one 13 x 9 x 2-inch baking pan.

In a bowl, sift together the flour, baking powder, and salt. Set aside.

Using an electric mixer, cream the butter, sugar, vanilla, and orange zest until light and fluffy. Add the eggs, one at a time, beating well after each addition.

Combine the orange juice and milk in a liquid measuring cup. Add the dry ingredients and the liquid alternately to the butter mixture, beating on low speed, until blended. Pour the batter into the prepared pans. Bake in the oven until a toothpick inserted in the center comes out clean, 30 to 35 minutes. Cool the cakes in their pans on a wire rack for 10 minutes. Then remove the cakes from the pans and allow to cool thoroughly.

Place one of the cake layers on a serving platter. Spread half of the buttercream evenly over the top. Place the second layer on top, and spread the remaining buttercream over it. **Serves 10 to 12**

## orange buttercream

4 tablespoons unsalted butter, room temperature

3 ounces cream cheese, room temperature

1½ cups sifted confectioner's sugar

Pinch of salt

1 tablespoon grated orange zest

In an electric mixer, beat the butter, cream cheese, confectioner's sugar, and salt until combined and smooth. Add the orange zest and mix together.

**Makes enough to frost cake**

# orange and crystallized ginger biscotti

*Biscotti* means "twice cooked" and refers to the ubiquitous dried cookie of Italy that is first baked, then sliced and baked again until crisp. These biscotti are flavored with grappa, an Italian brandy made from fermented grape pomace (pulp, skins, and seeds). Try dipping them in an after-dinner espresso or cappuccino, or in a glass of Vin Santo, a sweet dessert wine.

4 tablespoons unsalted butter, out of the refrigerator for 15 minutes

6 tablespoons sugar

1 egg

1 tablespoon grappa or brandy

2 tablespoons grated orange zest

¾ teaspoon orange extract

½ teaspoon ground cinnamon

2 teaspoons ground ginger

¼ cup chopped crystallized ginger

1 cup plus 2 tablespoons all-purpose flour

¾ teaspoon baking powder

⅛ teaspoon salt

¾ cup coarsely chopped pecans, toasted

Preheat the oven to 325°F.

In an electric mixer, cream the butter until smooth. Add the sugar and mix until light and fluffy. Add the egg and beat until smooth. Beat in the grappa, orange zest, orange extract, cinnamon, ginger, and crystallized ginger until well mixed.

In another bowl, sift together the flour, baking powder, and salt. Add the dry ingredients and the pecans to the creamed mixture, and mix together. The dough should not be sticky when you press your fingertips into it. If it is, add more flour, a teaspoon at a time.

On a lightly floured board, make 2 sausage-like rolls of dough, 1 inch in diameter. Set them 2 inches apart on a parchment-lined baking sheet, and bake in the top third of the oven for 20 to 25 minutes, or until lightly browned on top.

Slice the logs diagonally into ½-inch-thick cookies. Lay the cookies in a single layer on the baking sheet, and return to the oven. Bake until they feel dry and toasted, 10 to 20 minutes. Turn the cookies over and dry them on the other side, 10 to 20 minutes.

Cool the cookies on a wire rack. They can be stored for 2 weeks in an airtight container.                                                                   Makes 40 biscotti

# botrytis, or noble rot

Luck, poetry, boldness, commitment, skill, and a fungus called *Botrytis cinerea* combine to produce distinctive dessert wines that have been called "liquid gold."

*Botrytis cinerea* is a vine disease that can have either a disastrous or a beneficial effect on grapes, depending on the age at which it affects them. Almost ripe or slightly bruised grapes affected by botrytis will be severely damaged by a condition called gray rot. But in ripe, healthy, whole light-skinned grapes under favorable weather conditions, botrytis can develop in its benevolent form, called noble rot, and is responsible for some of the world's most extraordinary, long-lived, and complex sweet wines. Think of Château d'Yquem Sauternes.

Botrytized wines are made from white grapes affected by noble rot (Château d'Yquem is 100 percent botrytized).

The risks and costs involved in making botrytized wines are great and account for their high cost. Luck must be with the vintner, and specific (almost poetic-sounding) climate conditions must prevail: misty autumn mornings and warm afternoons. But it is the boldness of the winemaker to risk disaster that must also be present. It takes real commitment and skill to make repeated passes through the vineyard, handpicking the grapes at the optimum point of botrytis infection and then pressing them repeatedly to get the richer juices the botrytized grapes produce.

Sauternes, France, is the area that has the greatest chance of making a quantity of high-quality botrytized wines. But other countries are making an excellent try: Germany, Italy, Spain, Portugal, South Africa, Australia, New Zealand, and right here in the California wine country.

# italian almond crumb cookie

These "cookies," which are baked in a round cake pan and then cut into wedges, are traditional in the Veneto, where they're called *torta sbrisolona*. I had them there during a teaching assignment and begged for the recipe. Finally, after several days, my friends got it for me. The crumbliness comes from the almonds and polenta.

1⅓ cups all-purpose flour

½ cup coarse polenta

½ cup sugar

1 cup (¼ pound) ground almonds

1 teaspoon grated lemon zest

Pinch of salt

2 egg yolks

1 tablespoon rum

8 tablespoons (1 stick) unsalted butter, chilled

1 tablespoon confectioner's sugar

Preheat the oven to 350°F. Butter a 9-inch round springform pan.

In a food processor, pulse the flour, polenta, sugar, almonds, lemon zest, and salt until well mixed. Add the egg yolks and rum, and process until the mixture looks crumbly, 30 seconds. Add the butter and process just until it starts to look as if it would hold together.

Crumble the mixture evenly into the prepared pan, but do not press it down. Sprinkle the top with the confectioner's sugar. Bake in the oven until light golden, 40 to 45 minutes.

Remove the sides of the springform pan, and immediately cut the cookie into serving pieces. Serve warm or at room temperature.                    **Serves 8-10**

# polenta shortbread

Who doesn't like shortbread? And these are hard to beat: They contrast a wonderful melt-in-your-mouth delicacy with the crunch of polenta. You could use regular cornmeal, but polenta has more texture. Serve these with a bowl of vanilla ice cream, with Peach Granita (see page 309), or just by themselves.

> 1 cup (2 sticks) unsalted butter, room temperature
> ½ cup plus 1 tablespoon confectioner's sugar
> 1 teaspoon orange extract, Grand Marnier, or pure orange oil
> 1 tablespoon finely grated orange zest
> ½ teaspoon ground cardamom
> 1¾ cups all-purpose flour
> ½ cup polenta
> Pinch of salt

Using an electric mixer, cream the butter until light. Add the confectioner's sugar, orange extract, orange zest, and cardamom, and mix well. In another bowl, sift together the flour, polenta, and salt. Mix the dry ingredients into the creamed mixture to form a dough. Flatten the dough into a rough rectangle, and cut it in half. Wrap each piece in plastic wrap, and refrigerate for 1 hour.

Preheat the oven to 350°F. Line two baking sheets with baking parchment.

Working with 1 piece of dough at a time, roll the dough out until it is ⅜-inch thick and measures approximately 6 x 6 inches. Cut the dough into 1½- to 2-inch square cookies, refrigerating as necessary to keep the dough firm. Repeat with the second piece of dough.

Transfer the cookies to the prepared baking sheets, leaving space between them, and pierce each cookie with a fork. Bake until light brown, 15 to 18 minutes.

**Makes 24 cookies**

# first cookie

When I was about eight years old, I really wanted to make some cookies all by myself. They had to be oatmeal cookies—not chocolate chip, but oatmeal cookies. And my mother let me. I followed the recipe very carefully, measuring exactly as my Mom had taught me. I spooned the batter onto the cookie sheet and put the first batch in the oven.

While they cooked, I called out to my Mom that we would need to get more baking soda as I'd used the last of it. She said, "That's funny. I just bought a brand-new box." She came into the kitchen, looked at me, and then we both looked at the oven. Opening the oven door, we saw that there was now just one BIG cookie that covered the entire cookie sheet and was creeping over the sides. I had used 1½ *cups* of baking soda, not 1½ *teaspoons!*

But the very best part came when we took the giant out of the oven and broke off a piece. My Mom said, "You know? They're still good."

# scharffen berger meringue cookies

John Scharffenberger and Robert Steinberg returned to centuries-old techniques when they opened their Scharffen Berger chocolate factory in San Francisco. They start with the most select beans from around the world and roast them in small batches. The chocolate is incredibly rich and complex in flavor. Here I've mixed their bittersweet and semisweet chocolate with hazelnuts in a delicious meringue cookie.

> 2 cups shelled hazelnuts
>
> 3 egg whites
>
> 1 tablespoon white vinegar
>
> ¼ teaspoon salt
>
> 1 cup sugar
>
> Seeds from 1 vanilla bean
>
> 4 ounces Scharffen Berger bittersweet chocolate, finely chopped
>
> 4 ounces Scharffen Berger semisweet chocolate, finely chopped

Preheat the oven to 350°F.

Place the hazelnuts on a baking sheet and toast until the skins crack and the nuts are light golden, 10 to 15 minutes. Wrap the hazelnuts in a rough kitchen towel and rub to remove as much of the skins as possible. Chop coarsely, and reserve. Reduce the oven heat to 250°F.

In a bowl, beat the egg whites, vinegar, and salt until soft peaks form. Gradually add the sugar and the vanilla seeds, and continue to beat until the meringue forms stiff peaks. Gently fold in the chocolate and the hazelnuts.

Line three baking sheets with baking parchment. Drop the mixture by tablespoonfuls about 1 inch apart onto the lined sheets. Bake until firm, about 45 minutes. Cool on a wire rack. Store up to several days in an airtight container.     **Makes 60 cookies**

# mango and pink grapefruit sorbet

One of the best desserts, in my opinion, is sorbet: light and refreshing, good with any meal. I make this one with mangos and pink grapefruit, which are in season at the same time. The color is beautiful! The sorbet would be nice served with Polenta Shortbread (see page 298).

2 pink grapefruit

3 ripe mangos

1 cup sugar

1 tablespoon fresh lemon juice

With a zester, remove 1 tablespoon of the zest from one of the grapefruit. Reserve. Juice both grapefruit and reserve the juice.

Using a sharp knife, peel the mangos and cut the flesh away from the pit. Cut the flesh into small pieces.

Place the grapefruit juice and mango flesh in a blender, and puree on high speed until smooth. Strain through a fine-mesh strainer into a large measuring cup. You should have approximately 4 cups of puree. For each 4 cups of puree, measure 1 cup sugar.

Place approximately one-quarter of the puree and all of the sugar in a saucepan, and stir over medium heat until the sugar has dissolved. Rub a little of the juice between your fingers; when the sugar is melted and you can no longer feel the graininess, remove the pan from the heat. Stir the warm mixture into the remaining puree. Add the lemon juice and grapefruit zest and stir together. Chill until the mixture is cold.

Freeze according to the instructions for your ice cream maker.

To serve, scoop the sorbet into bowls.                    **Makes approximately 1 quart**

# strawberry rhubarb sorbet
# with strawberry sauce

Among the classic combinations—basil and tomatoes, chocolate and orange—is strawberries and rhubarb. They come into season at the same time in the spring, and the pair work well together in a sorbet. It's refreshing and has a great texture.

### Sorbet
¾ pound fresh rhubarb, cut into 1-inch lengths (about 4 cups)
2 tablespoons water
1½ pounds fresh strawberries, hulled and halved (5 to 6 cups)
1½ cups sugar

### Sauce
2 cups fresh strawberries, hulled and halved
2 tablespoons sugar
2 tablespoons Crème de Cassis (optional)

Combine the rhubarb and the water in a medium saucepan. Cover and cook over medium-high heat until the rhubarb starts to fall apart, 3 minutes. Remove the cover, reduce the heat to medium-low, and simmer until the rhubarb is very tender, 4 to 5 minutes. Set aside to cool for 10 to 15 minutes.

Puree the rhubarb and strawberries together in a blender until completely smooth. Strain through a fine-mesh strainer into a large measuring cup. You should have about 4 cups of puree. For each 4 cups of puree, measure 1½ cups sugar.

Pour approximately one-quarter of the puree into a small saucepan. Add the sugar and heat over medium-high heat until the mixture bubbles around the edges and the sugar is dissolved, 1 to 2 minutes. Stir this into the remaining puree, and refrigerate until well chilled.

Freeze the sorbet according to the instructions for your ice cream maker.

For the sauce, thirty minutes before serving, toss the strawberries, sugar, and Cassis together in a bowl.

To serve, scoop the sorbet into serving bowls and spoon the sauce over the top.

Serves 8

# caramelized pineapple with coconut sorbet

We all have a best friend. But who has a best *chef* friend? This delicious sorbet is the inspiration of my friend Gary Danko, chef and owner of Restaurant Gary Danko in San Francisco. It has incredible flavor and is so easy to make. You can garnish the sorbet with toasted flaked coconut.

**Coconut sorbet**
½ **vanilla bean**
½ **cup water**
¾ **cup sugar**
2 **cups unsweetened coconut milk (including the cream at the top of the can)**
**Pinch of salt**

**Pineapple**
2 **tablespoons unsalted butter**
¼ **cup packed light brown sugar**
6 **whole slices fresh pineapple, ¾ to 1 inch thick**
¼ **cup dark rum**
⅓ **cup heavy cream**
**Pinch of salt**

Prepare the sorbet: Split the vanilla bean and scrape the seeds from the pod. Discard the pod. In a bowl, combine the vanilla seeds, water, sugar, coconut milk, and salt, and stir until the sugar has dissolved. Freeze according to the directions for your ice cream maker.

For the pineapple, melt the butter in a large frying pan over high heat. Add the brown sugar and stir until it has melted, 1 minute. Add the pineapple slices in batches and cook until golden, 2 minutes per side. Add the rum. Light a match and carefully touch the match to the edge of the pan to create a flame. Carefully swirl the pan until the flames subside, 30 seconds. Add the cream and salt, and simmer until the cream thickens, 2 to 3 minutes.

To serve, place 1 slice of pineapple on each plate. Spoon some of the sauce over it, and top with a scoop of the coconut sorbet. **Makes about 3 cups sorbet; serves 6**

# vanilla

Vanilla beans are the long, thin seed pods of the vanilla orchid grown in Mexico, Madagascar, Tahiti, and Hawaii. At one point it was considered an aphrodisiac, and was so rare that it was reserved for royalty. Today, vanilla beans are relatively expensive due to the labor-intensive, time-consuming process of obtaining them. Look for vanilla beans that are soft and supple. The pods should be split in half lengthwise and the soft pastelike seeds scraped out with a small knife. Both the seeds and the pod are used for flavoring. Use the leftover pods to scent sugar, or steep them in a jar of vodka, brandy, or Cognac to make your own vanilla extract.

### VANILLA SUGAR
2 leftover pods, cut in half crosswise
Sugar

Place the vanilla beans in a jar and cover with sugar. Let stand for 2 weeks.

### VANILLA EXTRACT
2 leftover pods, cut in half crosswise
¾ cup vodka, brandy, or Cognac

Place the vanilla beans in a jar and cover with vodka, brandy, or Cognac. Let stand for 6 months. Strain.

# pineapple and meyer lemon sorbet

Winter is a challenging time to come up with a dessert. Of course, there are always citrus and pineapples! In my travels, I have noticed that more and more Meyer lemons have become available in the market, usually in January. A majority of Meyer lemons are grown in California, but they are also grown in Florida. They're sweeter, more floral-tasting lemons with bright, shiny yellow skin. If you cannot find them, substitute Eureka or Lisbon lemons, available year-round.

3 Meyer, Eureka, or Lisbon lemons
1 ripe pineapple, peeled, cored, and cut into chunks
1 cup sugar

Grate 2 tablespoons lemon zest and reserve. Juice the lemons and reserve the juice separately.

Place the lemon juice and the pineapple chunks in a blender and puree until smooth. Strain through a fine-mesh strainer into a large measuring cup. Add the reserved zest and stir together. You should have about 4 cups of puree. For each 4 cups of puree, measure 1 cup sugar.

Place approximately one-quarter of the puree in a saucepan. Add the sugar and stir over medium heat until the mixture is simmering and the sugar has melted. Add this to the remaining puree and stir together. Place in the refrigerator and chill until cold.

Freeze according to the instructions for your ice cream maker.

**Makes approximately 1 quart**

# cinnamon apple sorbet

The flavors of cinnamon, nutmeg, and Calvados, an apple brandy from Normandy, make this an ideal autumn dessert. It's very easy to make—almost like making applesauce and then freezing it. And the sorbet has an unbelievably creamy texture, without any cream at all.

4½ pounds Yellow Delicious apples, peeled, quartered, and cored

1 tablespoon fresh lemon juice

½ teaspoon ground cinnamon

Large pinch of freshly grated nutmeg

1 tablespoon water

1 cup sugar

1 to 2 tablespoons Calvados, brandy, or Cognac

In a soup pot, toss the apples with the lemon juice, cinnamon, and nutmeg. Add the water, cover, and simmer over medium-low heat until the apples are very soft and falling apart, 15 to 25 minutes.

Put the cooked apples into a blender and puree until completely smooth. Strain through a fine-mesh strainer into a large measuring cup. You should have approximately 4 cups of puree. For each 4 cups of apple puree, measure 1 cup sugar.

Combine approximately one-quarter of the apple puree and all of the sugar in a saucepan. Stir over medium heat until the sugar has dissolved. Rub a little of the juice between your fingers; when the sugar is melted and you can no longer feel the graininess, remove the pan from the heat. Stir the warm mixture into the remaining puree. Stir in the Calvados. Chill until the mixture is cold.

Freeze according to the instructions for your ice cream maker.

**Makes approximately 1 quart**

# peach granita with sugared rose petals

What, no ice cream machine? Here's the answer! Granita is a refreshing, icy cold, Italian slush made for hot summer days. I make this one with peaches, but you can use other seasonal fruits—melons, citrus fruits, nectarines, berries—or that Italian favorite, coffee.

Keep in mind that the sugared rose petals need two to three days to dry sufficiently. You can also sugar pansies or rose geranium leaves. Make sure the petals or leaves have not been sprayed or treated with any pesticides, or get them from an organic grower.

Sugared rose petals
2 egg whites
2 tablespoons water
1 cup very loosely packed rose petals, unsprayed
1 cup superfine sugar

Granita
5 medium (1½ pounds) ripe peaches, peeled and cut into chunks
1 cup water
1 cup sugar
1 tablespoon fresh lemon juice

In a small bowl, whisk the egg whites and water together lightly to break up the whites. Holding the base of each rose petal with tweezers, brush the egg wash on all surfaces of the petal.

Sprinkle with sugar, turning to coat the entire surface. Place on a waxed or parchment-lined baking sheet and set aside uncovered, at room temperature, turning occasionally, until dry and crisp, 1 to 2 days. Brush off any excess sugar.

For the granita, puree the peaches in a blender until smooth. Strain through a fine-mesh strainer into a large measuring cup. You should have approximately 2 cups of peach puree.

Mix the water and sugar in a saucepan, and heat over high heat until the sugar dis-

solves. Add the sugar syrup and the lemon juice to the peach puree. Pour the mixture into a shallow 13 x 9-inch metal or glass baking dish, and place in the freezer until ice crystals begin to form, 1½ to 2 hours. Whisk with a fork to break up the crystals. Continue to whisk with a fork every 30 minutes until the mixture is completely crystallized and like slush, another 2 hours total.

Spoon or scoop the granita into ice-cold serving dishes. Garnish with the rose petals, and serve immediately. **Serves 6**

# ginger ice cream with chocolate-covered almonds

My friend David Lebovitz, with whom I worked at Chez Panisse, gave me the inspiration for this rich homemade ice cream. Be sure to use fresh ginger, as it gives the ice cream a little hotness. The chocolate-covered almonds are delicious in the ice cream or on their own, just popped into your mouth. You could also use this ice cream to fill cream puffs or profiteroles, and pour the chocolate sauce on top.

Ice cream
One 3-inch piece fresh ginger root (about 2½ ounces), peeled and thinly sliced
1½ cups heavy cream
1½ cups milk
¾ cup sugar
6 egg yolks

Chocolate sauce and almonds
½ cup sugar
½ cup unsweetened cocoa powder, preferably Dutch-process
½ cup water
¼ cup heavy cream
¼ cup light corn syrup
1 ounce bittersweet chocolate, chopped into small pieces
1 tablespoon unsalted butter

Chocolate-covered almonds
1 cup blanched almonds
5 ounces bittersweet chocolate

Prepare the ice cream: Place the ginger in a small saucepan and cover with water. Over high heat, bring to a boil and simmer for 2 minutes. Drain, and discard the water. Combine the ginger, cream, milk, and sugar in a large saucepan. Bring almost to a boil over medium-high heat, stirring occasionally. Remove from the heat and let stand for 2 hours.

Place the egg yolks in a large bowl. Scald the cream mixture again. Then slowly add the hot cream mixture to the yolks, drop by drop, whisking constantly. When all of the cream mixture has been added, pour the mixture back into the saucepan and place it over medium heat. Immediately start scraping the bottom and sides of the pan with a flat-edged wooden spoon or with a heatproof spatula. Cook until the mixture begins to thicken and coats the back of a wooden spoon; it should register no higher than 170°F. Strain the mixture through a fine-mesh strainer into a clean bowl. Whisk very quickly to cool the mixture. Place the mixture in the refrigerator and cool completely.

Meanwhile, prepare the chocolate sauce: Whisk the sugar and cocoa together in a saucepan. Whisk in the water until blended. Bring to a simmer over medium-high heat. Remove the pan from the heat and immediately stir in the cream, corn syrup, chocolate, and butter. Stir until the chocolate has melted, 1 to 2 minutes. Set aside.

For the chocolate-covered almonds, preheat the oven to 350°F.

Place the almonds on a baking sheet and bake until golden brown, 5 to 7 minutes. Allow to cool.

Coarsely chop the chocolate and place it in a double boiler or in a bowl set over a pan of boiling water to melt. When the chocolate has melted, add the almonds and stir together. Spread the chocolate and almonds onto a parchment-lined baking sheet, and let cool completely. When the chocolate is cool and set, place it on a cutting board and coarsely chop.

Freeze the ice cream according to the instructions for your ice cream maker. Toward the last 2 minutes of churning, add the chocolate-covered almonds.

To serve, gently warm the chocolate sauce in a saucepan. Scoop the ice cream into bowls, and drizzle with the chocolate sauce.

**Makes 1 generous quart ice cream; 1½ cups chocolate sauce**

# chocolate, cinnamon, and orange ice cream

The combination of flavors in this ice cream inspires images of Spain, to which Columbus first brought cocoa beans over 500 years ago. It has an incredibly smooth texture that is achieved by adding the hot ice cream base to finely chopped, not melted, chocolate.

2 cups milk

2 cups heavy cream

¾ cup sugar

Zest of 3 oranges

5 cinnamon sticks, 3 inches long

4 ounces bittersweet chocolate, finely chopped

3 ounces semisweet chocolate, finely chopped

9 egg yolks

Candied orange peel (optional)

2 oranges

1⅔ cups sugar

⅓ cup water

Combine the milk, cream, sugar, orange zest, and cinnamon sticks in a large saucepan over medium heat. Heat until bubbles form around the edges and the sugar has melted. Remove from the heat and let sit for 2 hours.

Place the two chocolates in a large bowl and set aside.

In another bowl, whisk together the egg yolks. Scald the milk mixture again. Add the hot mixture to the egg yolks, little by little, whisking constantly. Pour the mixture back into the saucepan. Over medium heat, stir constantly until it thickens enough to coat the back of the spoon. Immediately strain through a fine-mesh strainer into the bowl containing the chocolate. Whisk until the chocolate has melted. Place in the refrigerator and chill until ice-cold.

For the candied orange peel, use a vegetable peeler to remove the zest from the 2 oranges, making the longest strips possible. Be sure to avoid peeling the white pith. If necessary, place the orange peel on a work surface, pith side up, and use a sharp paring knife to scrape the pith away. Cut the peel into thin diagonal strips measuring 2 inches long and $\frac{1}{16}$ inch wide.

Combine $\frac{2}{3}$ cup of the sugar and the water in a saucepan. Cover and bring to a simmer over medium heat. Simmer until the sugar has dissolved, 30 seconds. Add the orange peel, cover, and simmer for 3 minutes. Remove from the heat and let cool completely. Remove the peel from the syrup and let it drain on paper towels.

Place the remaining 1 cup sugar on a baking sheet. Toss the drained peel in the sugar, separating the pieces.

Freeze the ice cream according to the directions for your ice cream maker.

To serve, scoop the ice cream into individual serving bowls and garnish with the candied orange peel. Makes 1½ quarts

*Note: To store the candied orange peel, layer the pieces in sugar in a covered container. It will keep indefinitely in the refrigerator.*

# yogurt and spiced walnuts
# drizzled with honey

In Greece and the Middle East, yogurt is used a great deal, even for dessert. And what could be simpler than this: You just drain the yogurt, spread it on a plate, and then drizzle it with honey and nuts. Try to find chestnut honey; it's an excellent, very aromatic honey made by bees that feed on chestnut flowers. It used to be available only in Italy, but now I see it in specialty stores.

4 cups full-fat yogurt

½ cup walnut halves

1 tablespoon walnut oil

2 teaspoons sugar

¼ teaspoon ground cardamom

Pinch of ground allspice

6 tablespoons honey, preferably chestnut

Place the yogurt in a sieve lined with paper towels or cheesecloth and set the sieve over a bowl. Let the yogurt drain for 4 hours.

Meanwhile, preheat the oven to 375°F.

Toss the walnuts with the walnut oil, sugar, cardamom, and allspice. Place the nuts on a baking sheet and toast until they darken slightly, 5 to 7 minutes. Remove from the oven and allow to cool. Chop the walnuts coarsely.

Divide the yogurt among six dessert plates, and with the back of a spoon, spread it over the surface of each plate. Drizzle each plate with 1 tablespoon of the honey. Sprinkle the walnuts over the yogurt, and serve.

Serves 6

# index

(Page numbers in *italic* refer to illustrations.)

sweet and hot, grilled
chicken salad with olives
and, 180–82, *181*
wood-fired vegetable salad
with tomatoes, onions,
olives and, 44–46, *45*
yellow, roasted corn, tomato
and, soup, 92–93
pimentos, smoked, Spanish
omelette with, 47
pineapple:
caramelized, with coconut
sorbet, 305
and Meyer lemon sorbet, 307
pine nuts:
fettuccine with Gorgonzola
and, 74
layered salad of bulgur,
fennel, dill, mint and,
155–56
rolled grape leaves with rice,
feta, currants and, 37–38
toasting, 154
wilted greens with raisins,
fried bread and, 39–40, *40*
Pinot Noir, 113
pita:
crisps, 101–2, *102*
crisps with spinach, walnut,
and garlic puree, 32–33
*fattoush*, 142–43, *143*
pizza:
crispy cracker, with
mahogany onions, 57–58
dough, best, 54
equipment for, 53
with leeks, Gorgonzola, and
walnuts, 52–54
with red-hot spiced lamb
and tomatoes, Turkish,
55–56, *56*

plum(s):
honey-poached, with
mascarpone, 265
stone fruit summer salad,
126, *127*
polenta:
Italian almond crumb
cookie, 296, *297*
shortbread, 298
triangles, crisp, 241
pomegranates, salad of grapes,
apples, pears, pecans and,
with frisée, 157
potato(es):
lemon and garlic-roasted,
238
new, and green garlic soup,
106–7
roasted, with tomatoes and
garlic mayonnaise, 41–42
preserved lemons, 193–94
prosciutto:
chicken rolled with fontina,
sage and, 179
sugar snap pea and mint
salad with, 159
-wrapped greens with hot
pepper and garlic, 36
prunes, in sauce of poached
fruits, Riesling, thyme,
and honey, 255–57, *256*
pudding, bread, with berries,
summer, 251–52
puff pastry, quick, 50–51
purslane, in *fattoush*, 142–43,
*143*

radicchio:
chopped salad, 145
risotto with Zinfandel and,
72–73

raisins, wilted greens with pine
nuts, fried bread and, 39–
40, *40*
raspberry(ies):
almond cake with, three-
minute, 278–79
and fig clafouti, 262
ravioli:
red onion, with thyme
cream, 75–76
spinach, with tomatoes and
basil, 185–87
rhubarb strawberry sorbet
with strawberry sauce,
303–4
rice:
"olives," 68–69
rolled grape leaves with feta,
currants, pine nuts and,
37–38
*see also* risotto
ricotta cheese, in Italian torta
rustica, 203–5, *205*
ricotta salata, herbed, penne
with tomatoes and, 190
Riesling, sauce of poached
fruits, thyme, honey and,
semolina custards with,
255–57, *256*
risotto, 71
croquettes with mozzarella,
70–71
with oven-roasted tomatoes
and basil, 188–89
with Zinfandel and
radicchio, 72–73
romaine salad with oranges,
walnuts, and Manchego,
152–54, *153*
*romesco*, garlic shrimp with,
81–82